The Urban Gardener

The Urban Gardener

HOW TO GROW THINGS
SUCCESSFULLY ON BALCONIES,
TERRACES, DECKS, AND
ROOFTOPS

Sonia Day

KEY PORTER BOOKS

National Library of Canada Cataloguing in Publication Data

Day, Sonia

    The urban gardener : how to grow things successfully on balconies, terraces, decks, and rooftops / Sonia Day

Includes index.

ISBN 1-55263-546-5

1. Balcony gardening. 2. Roof gardening. I. Title.

SB419.5.D38   2003   635.9'671   C2002-905367-6

THE CANADA COUNCIL | LE CONSEIL DES ARTS
FOR THE ARTS | DU CANADA
SINCE 1957 | DEPUIS 1957

ONTARIO ARTS COUNCIL
CONSEIL DES ARTS DE L'ONTARIO

The publisher gratefully acknowledges the support of the Canada Council for the Arts and the Ontario Arts Council for its publishing program.

We acknowledge the financial support of the Government of Canada through the Book Publishing Industry Development Program (BPIDP) for our publishing activities.

Key Porter Books Limited
70 The Esplanade
Toronto, Ontario
Canada M5E 1R2
www.keyporter.com

Text design: Peter Maher
Illustrations: Jock MacRae
Electronic formatting: Heidy Lawrance Associates

Printed and bound in Canada
03 04 05 06 07 08 6 5 4 3 2 1

For Sue Martin

Contents

Introduction

Gardens are getting smaller. Only a few years ago, you needed a house with a front and back yard to qualify as a *real* gardener.

Not any more. People no longer confess in apologetic terms that "I just have a balcony." In fact, growing things on balconies —and rooftops, townhouse terraces, decks, and patios—has become North America's hottest gardening trend

What's driving this change is, of course, demographics. More and more of us are living alone, and in cities. Many older couples are leaving family homes behind and buying condominiums. Younger twosomes, busy with careers and kids, are also coming to the conclusion that they don't have the time or the inclination to maintain a conventional garden, with an expanse of lawn and flowerbeds. While establishing a link with Mother Nature remains an ideal for most of us, we want that link to be small—and manageable.

Surprisingly, gardening magazines have been slow to recognize our changing attitudes to the great green world. Their features continue to focus on gardens around houses. Big gardens, mostly. There is very little material geared to the folks for whom the word "garden" means a collection of pots and planters grouped on a balcony or terrace. And while you can find plenty of books on container gardening, even these are often aimed at the "traditional" gardener—that is, they describe how to grow plants in containers around houses: on decks and patios, next to driveways, or on porches. The urban gardener who lives in a condo, apartment or townhouse tends to be forgotten.

Hence this book. It explains not only how to grow plants in containers, but also all the other nitty-gritty aspects of gardening off the ground. You'll learn how to get started when even the soil for your garden has to be hauled up elevators. There's advice on what will work on cold, windy balconies, where to buy plants when you don't have a car, how to create a quick and colorful instant garden, and how to help your little green oasis survive when winter comes. I've included money-saving ideas because so many condo and apartment dwellers don't have big budgets for gardening, particularly when they first move in. And there are lots of practical tips from real live city people who garden in small spaces.

An apartment dweller I met recently, Wendy Humphries, complained rather plaintively that "No one ever writes anything for us." After struggling for years with a balcony ten stories off the ground, she had finally managed to transform this space into her dream: a delightful urban retreat, overflowing with flowers and greenery, where she could sit with a glass of wine in the evening and feel surrounded by nature. Fulfilling this dream hadn't been easy, however. Wendy found many of her initial plant choices didn't survive—and she'd been ready, on occasion, to give up gardening.

"It would have been helpful to have a book for guidance," she mused, "because it is so different growing things above the ground."

It is indeed. Wendy, here is that book. Finally.

Those Bewildering Terms Gardeners Use

You won't find many in this book, but for the sake of brevity and clarity, a few horticultural expressions do pop up here and there. Here's what they mean.

Annual: A plant that grows from seed for only one summer, then dies.

Biennial: A plant that lasts two years. The first year, it usually sends out leaves, the second it produces flowers and seeds.

Bolt: When plants shoot up too quickly, they "bolt." Usually applied to leafy vegetables such as lettuce.

Cell paks: Little plastic trays, divided into compartments, in which pre-started plants are sold.

Deadhead: To snip off (or snap off with fingers) flower heads after they've bloomed. Done to encourage the plant to send out more flowers.

Double: Usually used in reference to flowers. Means two layers of petals, rather than one.

Hardy: Means plants can stay outside over the winter.

Mulch: A protective layer piled up around the base of plants to help them cope with winter or dryness.

Perennial: A plant that keeps coming up year after year.

Pinch: Remove buds. Usually applied to the little buds that form at the tips of plant stems.

Self-seed: When plants drop seeds at random, without any human help.

Single: Flowers that have only one layer of petals.

Spent: Has nothing to do with finances. Means a flower that has finished blooming.

Variegated: Usually used in reference to foliage. Means two (or more) different colors on the same leaf.

Weeping: Branches that hang downwards from a strong central stem. Usually used in reference to trees or shrubs.

Starting Out: Plan, If You Can

When it comes to gardening in small spaces, most of us do things back to front. We buy a condominium (or rent an apartment) and only start thinking about the outdoor space *after* we've moved in. Then we discover the drawbacks. That much-anticipated balcony (or terrace, or courtyard, or rooftop), which seemed so exciting at the outset, proves to have all kinds of inadequacies that we hadn't considered. It's too small, it gets no sun at all, it's windy, it faces an ugly air-conditioning shaft, there's no privacy, building management has all kinds of rules about what we can do there, and so on.

The way to avoid these kinds of disappointments is to think ahead. First of all, figure out why you want a little garden in the first place. Are you a serious gardener (or intending to be one)? Will you want to grow lots of plants out there? Or will you be content with a couple of flowerpots? Do you like sitting outside? Do you plan to relax quietly by yourself on the balcony—or do lots of entertaining? Then, before plunking down your hard-earned cash for the unit, check carefully that the exterior space is going to provide the amenities you want (or at least some of them).

That said, there's probably no such thing as a "perfect outdoor space." From a gardening point of view, however, some are much better designed than others. The most challenging kind of balcony is unfortunately all too common on many modern condominium and apartment buildings. It consists of a concrete pad jutting out from the building wall, with a railing running around three sides. The principal problem is that it's too open. There are no side walls on which to attach things, like trellises and hanging baskets. Often the difficulties are compounded by a solid wall of windows or glass patio doors directly behind the balcony. (You can't hang anything from those, either.) As well, most of these balconies are simply too small. There's hardly room for a chair, let alone flowerpots and planters. And it's often very windy.

Another important aspect that architects don't consider is watering arrangements. In condos and apartments, washrooms and kitchens are invariably situated far from the balcony or courtyard. Outside faucets never seem to be part of the deal, which means hauling heavy, clumsy watering cans over furniture, carpets, and hardwood flooring, often ruining everything in the process.

Not many of us have the financial wherewithal to shop around for a condominium or apartment with a custom-built balcony that's designed with gardening in mind. However, you can save yourself a lot of frustration by considering a few factors in advance.

What to look for in a balcony or courtyard

❀ **Space:** Good balconies (or townhouse courtyards) are roomy. An ideal size is 8 ft./2.5 m by 16 ft./5 m or bigger. A workable one is 6 ft./2 m by 6 ft./2 m.

❀ **Depth:** Avoid long, narrow spaces. It's difficult to fit chairs in them and awkward to move around them.

❀ **Surrounding walls:** Does the balcony or courtyard have any? The best type of balcony is partly inset into the sides of the building so you have solid walls on which to attach hooks and fixtures. (But it shouldn't have a roof overhanging the entire balcony, because that will stop the light getting in.) Townhouse courtyards are easier to work with if they have some kind of fence separating each unit.

❀ **Built-in planters:** Some buildings include them—and they are a tremendous plus because they make it possible to garden on different levels, instead of having to put everything on the floor of the balcony or courtyard.

❀ **Ground-floor lockers:** Does the unit have one, and is it accessible? Gardening in a small space inevitably involves finding space to stash a lot of stuff: bags of grow mix, planters, patio furniture, hoses. This storage area should be easy to reach.

❀ **Watering:** How far away is the nearest faucet? If you're buying a condo that hasn't been built yet, ask if it's possible to have a faucet installed on the balcony or in the courtyard as a custom feature. It will be worth every penny.

❀ **Building codes and bylaws:** Never presume that they won't affect you. Rules vary widely, and there are often restrictions on the type of gardening you can do. Some management boards forbid installation of any fixtures, like planters, trellises, and hanging baskets. Others don't allow residents to grow vegetables or certain kinds of vines and other plants. Always check that what you have in mind is going to be permitted.

❀ **Liability:** Add something to your balcony and you immediately become financially responsible for any damage that results from its installation. If your lovely new wooden planter leaks water onto the balcony below, staining the owner's posh white wicker chairs, you pay. Ditto if you install outdoor lighting in a courtyard and the wiring causes a fire in the unit next door. Always use qualified tradespeople if you make any structural changes—and first get permission to do the work.

> **Hot tip**
>
> "Carrying patio furniture down to lockers in the fall is back-breaking work. Buy tables and chairs that can stay outside all winter. Teak and lightweight cast aluminum are best, if you can afford them."
>
> —*Sue Martin, balcony gardener*

Let there be light (preferably lots)

You've moved in. You're dying to get started growing something. What to do first?

Look at the light outside. Carefully. Does your growing space have sun? Shade? A mixture of the two? It's important to find out. One of the biggest mistakes that beginning gardeners make is to march out and buy a lot of plants without working out how much light—and what *kind* of light—they have. When plant labels say, "Needs full sun," they generally mean at least six hours of unobstructed sunshine a day. If you don't have that much, it may be a waste of time and money to buy many sun-loving annuals and perennials. (However, there are lots of other things you can grow. See pages 55–56 and page 67.)

Before buying anything, observe carefully the time of day when the sun strikes your balcony, rooftop, or courtyard—and when it moves on. Also bear in mind that the sun shifts its position throughout the summer. By the end of June, it's going to rise and set much farther north than it does when you first venture outside after the winter.

Watch for obstructions that reduce the amount of light. Is your balcony (like so many) shaded much of the day by the balcony above? Do surrounding buildings or privacy fences stop the sun from reaching your courtyard terrace? And what about trees? Are they going to leaf out and cast shade once summer comes? It's crucial to consider all these factors because light—or the lack of it—will inevitably affect what you can grow.

Don't be discouraged, however, if your unit turns out to have more shade than you originally thought. Nowadays, people with shady balconies and courtyards are sometimes better off than those with supposedly "ideal" situations: unobstructed and facing smack south. With global warming becoming a reality, our summers are getting hotter. As a consequence, some high-rise gardeners are finding that a southern aspect is more of a hindrance than a help. Up high, the dry, searing heat becomes too much of a good thing for plants: they actually get sunburned.

There are no hard and fast rules about the best location for a balcony. It depends a lot on the local climate. Generally speaking, gardeners prefer balconies that face southeast or simply east. West is also good (but less so). However—here's the surprise—some balcony green thumbs, particularly those high off the ground, find their plants do surprisingly well on north-facing balconies. While they may not have any direct sunshine, there's still sufficient light up there—often bouncing off other buildings—for plants to flourish. Because pots and planters aren't baking every day in the sun's relentless rays, they don't dry out as quickly. The plants have a chance to establish healthy root systems and foliage.

Getting floored

Many balcony floors are made of concrete, which over time crumbles, flakes, and looks dreadful. One option is to paint the floor (if your building permits it). Use a paint designed specifically for concrete and a color that will blend in well with city dirt, such as gray. Avoid very dark colors; footprints and water stains will show, and you'll be forever wiping them off.

Some balcony gardeners find indoor-outdoor carpeting practical and comfortable (choose a muted shade, not that lurid rec room green), but don't make the carpet a permanent fixture. Left outside over the winter, this kind of floor covering will wreck the concrete. Also, be careful about water dripping from your plants onto the carpet. You don't want to be coping with mold and funny smells.

Another option is modular wooden or resin flooring that's made in squares. These sections are usually 2 ft./60 cm by 2 ft./60 cm and you simply slot them together on the floor. They're durable, look attractive, and come in all kinds of colors. They can also be custom-made to fit your space.

In courtyards and on rooftops you'll often get concrete paving slabs, which are functional but utilitarian. If the slabs aren't too big, swapping them for something else (like bricks, slate, or stone) can make a world of difference. On asphalt-covered rooftops, it's a good idea to lay a false roof on top—made from wooden crosspieces and raised on a framework of two-by-fours. Some gardeners also like to layer pebbles underneath planters and pots on rooftops to help drainage. Be sure to check with the management of your building, however, before doing any of these things. All kinds of restrictions are often imposed, usually for safety reasons. For example, some buildings won't permit the floor level on balconies and rooftops to be raised by even an inch because of concerns that someone may then topple over the balcony railing or rooftop parapet.

When you install wooden flooring or trellises, make all of it portable, lightweight, and easy to dismantle. Condo and apartment building bigwigs are fond of sending out edicts in spring announcing, "Everything must be removed from balconies and courtyards in order to carry out structural repairs." You don't want to be stuck with lugging a whole lot of heavy wooden planks and planters into your unit, and then keeping them indoors for months until the repairs are finished.

Tools to buy

One big plus of gardening on a balcony, terrace, or rooftop is that you don't have to invest in a lot of expensive equipment (unlike those poor suckers down below with their lawn mowers and string trimmers). You do need:

❀ Containers, of course (see pages 24–31).

❀ A hand trowel. Pick one with a narrow blade. If you want to remove a certain plant from a container, wide-bladed trowels tend to disturb other plants. The "slim Jims" are also best when making holes in growing mix in the spring for small plants.

❀ A fork or other small garden scratching tool. This is helpful for aerating impacted soil (so that water can get in) and for hooking out weeds. For really big planters, also buy a spade with a short handle. (If you don't have much storage space, camping stores sell spades with folding handles.)

- 🌸 Lightweight pruners. There are all kinds on the market. Since you're unlikely to get into heavy pruning sessions, go for inexpensive ones. (On a balcony, buy a safety strap too. See page 120.)
- 🌸 A big kitchen spoon, which is easier than a trowel for removing excess soil from pots or fitting soil around plants.
- 🌸 A brush and dustpan to keep things tidy.
- 🌸 A big plastic dishwashing bowl for potting up plants.
- 🌸 A cheap plastic spray bottle for concocting bug deterrents.
- 🌸 Thick-gauge garbage bags, which are great for storing excess soil, old plants, and discarded pots.
- 🌸 Gloves, if you don't like getting your hands dirty.
- 🌸 An out-of-sight storage area, if you have room for one. A chest with a lid is good: it can double as a bench.
- 🌸 Watering equipment (see pages 42–45).

Should you do a design?

Nowadays, gardening gurus blather on about "design." Their insistence that we should always plan everything—and follow all kinds of rules—has taken a lot of the fun out of growing things.

The truth is, you don't have to care a fig about design—or make complicated drawings—to become a gardener. Just go out and get started: buy a couple of containers, a bag of growing mix, a few plants, and maybe some easy-to-grow seeds. Pot your purchases up and watch what happens. The thrill of seeing a seed sprout—or a tiny bundle of leaves evolve into a lovely flower—is what hooks most people on gardening in the

Cheapie tools are fine

Lightweight trowels and small garden forks made of a material called Nyglass are perfect for container gardeners. They cost peanuts, they're tough, and they won't rust if you leave them out in the rain. They come in colors like black, brown, and green and are sold everywhere.

first place. Agonizing endlessly about the style you want, the "right" things to buy, and where to put everything is tedious and often a waste of time because once you begin to garden, you'll keep changing your mind anyway.

Here are some tips for those who do like to work from a plan:

Do

✓ Position patio furniture first. Make room for at least one small chair so you can sit and admire your handiwork. If you like entertaining and the balcony is big enough, you'll need a proper seating area.

✓ Start small. Buy a few cheap plastic pots, all the same color. Fill them with plants that are carefree. It's easy to go overboard and come home with too much. Then gardening becomes a chore, not a pleasure.

✓ Create a potscape. Group containers closely together, rather than dib-dobbing them along the balcony. They generally look better in threes and fives, instead of twos. (However, by all means break the "rules." A pair of pots containing matching shrubs or trees can look great in certain situations.)

✓ Find ways to place pots on different levels. Elevate one on a box. Tuck two others of differing heights on the floor in front of those. Hang up a fourth above the group. Avoid putting pots all the same size in a long, boring row.

✓ Decide on an "anchor" color, then find ways to keep introducing it to your planting scheme. For example, using burgundy as the anchor, include at least one flower with petals or centers in burgundy (maybe pots too); add a vine with burgundy-colored leaves like sweet potato vine *Ipomoea batatas* 'Blackie' or tradescantia *T. pallida purpurea*. Then echo the theme again with a coleus that has a burgundy streak running through it.

✔ Create a focal point. On a small balcony, this could be: a flower that's scarlet, shocking pink, or orange (like a geranium); a foliage plant with striking leaves; an interesting container; a tall or colorful ornament; a mini-fountain.

✔ Have a focal point that's off-center. Smack in the middle of the balcony is not usually the best position. Place pots so they lead your eye to the focal point.

✔ Remember that cool colors recede, while warm ones pop out. To create a feeling of distance in a small space, place flowers and foliage in blues, cool pinks, purples, and blue greens at the back. Position the reds, yellows, and orangey pinks at the front.

Don't

✘ Feel you have to follow any design rules or master plan.

✘ Buy a certain type of container, garden furniture, or plant just because it's trendy. Put your own personality into what you do.

✘ Clutter the space up with too many itsy-bitsy doodads.

✘ Place anything where you—or visitors—will trip over it.

✘ Try to tackle everything in one day.

The problem of privacy

Homes are getting smaller; so are outdoor spaces. In cities, more and more of us now live cheek by jowl with neighbors. That can be both a pleasure and a pain in the neck. If nosy Neetha and garrulous Greg are getting on your nerves, consider putting up privacy screens. Don't, however make this partition into a Berlin Wall (that is, completely solid). On balconies and roof-tops—and even in ground-floor courtyards—the air needs to be able to pass through the screen, or gusts of wind will cause continual problems for you—and those annoying people next door.

Simple, inexpensive screens can be made with ready-made sections of lattice (sold at home renovation stores). If you install a wood fence (on each side of a courtyard, for instance), make sure there is some air space between the slats. The "blocky" appearance of such barricades can be softened by a variety of climbing vines (see pages 90–95) and tall shrubs (see pages 96–101).

(see pages 90–95) and tall shrubs (see pages 96–101).

Hot to Pot:
Choosing the Right Containers

When looking for pots, think "practical" rather than "pretty." Even though gardening is booming, good containers are often hard to find. The problem with many is that they simply aren't big enough. The pot may look appealing gussied up with a couple of fake gerberas in the garden decor shop, but take it home and you'll discover that there's hardly room to squeeze a couple of trowelfuls of soil into it.

How to shop for pots

Companies that service the landscaping trade are often good places to find practical containers. (Look in the Yellow Pages. You can sometimes persuade these places to sell retail too.) Hardware and home renovation stores usually have Plain Jane pots that work well with outdoor plants. The choice at garden centers, once dismal, is improving. Check out ads in gardening magazines and sites for gardeners on the Web: you can sometimes find splendid containers for sale by mail order. Artists at craft fairs can also be good sources, because they often garden themselves and know what makes a good pot.

Before buying, ask yourself these questions:

❀ What do I want to grow in this pot?
❀ Is it suitable for the purpose?
❀ Will it blend in with what's already on my balcony?

Do

✓ Look for *deep* pots if you plan to grow perennials, vines, shrubs, and trees. Most need room for roots to spread.

✓ Choose shallow pots for drought-tolerant, succulent plants like echeverias and sedums. Filled with soil, they'll be lighter than bigger pots (and the less heavy stuff you have to haul upstairs, the better).

✓ Make sure there's a drainage hole. Some potters have the annoying habit of producing lovely ceramic creations that don't have a hole in the bottom.

✓ Buy pots that you find appealing. You're going to be seeing a lot of each other on the balcony.

✓ Consider a pot's portability. Does it weigh a ton already? Will you be able to carry it into the elevator—and along building corridors? How heavy will it be full of potting mix?

✓ Stick to small pots if you have a tiny space. Big ones will make it seem cramped.

✓ Think about how the pot will look with something planted in it. (Jazzy designs and doodads on pots can be cute at first glance, but they often detract from the plants—and you'll tire of them quickly.)

✓ Pick pots in several sizes. Some tall, some short, some wide make an attractive grouping. Mix oblong shapes with round ones.

✓ Put sets of wheels underneath big containers so you can move them easily. Many garden centers sell kits that consist of a frame on which

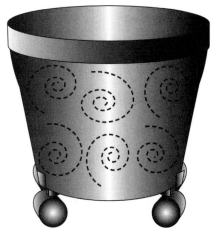

to stand the pot, with castors underneath. If you're handy, attach some castors (the kind that are used on furniture) to the bottom of pots yourself.

✓ Investigate the possibility of having planters built in if you want to grow big trees or shrubs. It's expensive but worth it. Insulate the planter interiors with Styrofoam sheeting in colder climates—and be sure to include a drainage hole.

✓ Use offbeat containers. Old boots, olive oil and paint cans, or asparagus boxes from the greengrocer all can look terrific. A hot trend in Europe is to stand pots inside bags. Garden designers are using burlap sacks, old cloth shoulder bags, and even (yikes) grocery bags from the supermarket. These funky touches are fun, but don't overdo them.

✓ Be bold and original. Try painting your pots. Most containers—clay, plastic, wood, or synthetic materials—can take paint well. (Use a glossy oil-based paint that resists dampness. Paint before you put the plant in.) Try signal red, hot pink, canary yellow, Provençal blue, or purple, then choose plants that echo those colors. Bear in mind, though, that hot hues aren't restful. If you want a peaceful retreat, choose muted shades. Steel gray looks good with anything and is an excellent backdrop to many flowers, particularly pink and white ones.

Don't

✗ Buy pots that look great but have thick sides and tiny interiors. Inspect both the inside and outside. Pots that are wide at the top but very narrow at the bottom are a no-no. They'll cramp roots.

✗ Have too many styles and colors, especially if your balcony is small. Pots with a unified theme look best.

✗ Buy pots that have ornamental bits and pieces stuck on their sides. Soil and city dirt gets trapped in the raised areas, and they are difficult to clean. Remember also that white pots get grubby quickly.

✗ Go overboard. It's easy to buy too many containers and then find you don't have the energy, funds, or space to fill them with plants.

Which container works best?

Different materials suit different purposes. Ultimately, containers are also a matter of personal taste. Here are some pot pointers:

Ceramic and glass

Pluses: Often have great textures and colors. Show off plants nicely. Containers called "jardinieres" are usually made of ceramic. They don't dry out as quickly as clay.

Minuses: Heavy. Break easily. Many don't have drainage holes.

Recommendations: Avoid, but if you have a gorgeous ceramic jardiniere, nestle a plastic pot containing the plant inside it on a layer of gravel.

Clay

Pluses: Classic. Looks great, ages nicely, and is porous, so plants can breathe through it. Some gardeners swear that many plants, particularly herbs, grow better in clay—and they refuse to use any other kind of pot. Glazed clay pots won't dry out as quickly.

Minuses: Heavy. Breaks easily. Plants need watering more often. Cracks in frost, so you have to empty pots every fall.

Recommendation: For purists. Soak pots before planting. Skip strawberry jars (They have holes in their sides and dry out too quickly.) Look for clay pots that are fired at very high temperatures and are therefore less likely to crack. Skip clay if you want a low-maintenance garden.

Concrete and stone

Pluses: Formal. Elegant. Good for big things like trees and shrubs.

Minuses: Concrete can crack and crumble in frost. Heavy. Not portable.

Recommendations: Good for ground-floor courtyards only—unless they're already built into your balcony.

Metal

Pluses: Hip, contemporary. Also classic. (Aluminum florists' buckets and bronze or iron urns are hot in some circles.) Shiny surfaces look chic against brick walls, add sparkle to gloomy balconies, and show off some plants well.

Minuses: Expensive. Can rust. Corrodes. (Aluminum won't rust, but dents easily.) Can be heavy. Salts and minerals in water make sides look scummy.

Recommendations: If you like metal, use it for all your containers. Don't mix metal with other materials.

Plastic

Pluses: Lightweight. Cheap. Retains moisture. Terra cotta–colored plastic pots look as good as clay ones.

Minuses: Plastic can get too hot—and may fry plants in heat waves. Flimsy. May blow over in windy areas.

Recommendations: Best choice for budget gardeners. Pick light colors. Dark shades, like green and black, soak up more heat.

Resin, fiberglass, and other synthetic materials

Pluses: Lightweight. Tough. Durable. Terrific styles and sizes. Some now look exactly like "the real thing"—i.e., stone troughs, antique urns, terra cotta.

Minuses: Pricey. Expect to pay up to $200 for a big container. Tall ones can blow over in windy locations.

Recommendations: Best choice for balcony gardeners, if you can afford them.

Wood

Pluses: Nice appearance, natural looking, insulates plants well, keeps roots cool. Can be painted to a color you want or covered in materials like copper sheeting. Good for big, built-in planters. A group in redwood, cedar, or teak gives continuity, especially in a small space.

Minuses: Cheap ones are inclined to rot. Treated wood lasts longer but is toxic. Often leaks, unless seams are well sealed.

Recommendation: Raise wooden planters off the ground on supports or legs so air can pass underneath. Line wooden containers with plastic and nestle plastic pots containing plants inside.

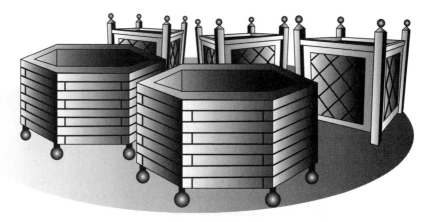

Go for good pots

It's worth investing in quality containers. Be selective. Wait till the fall, when the expensive resin ones go on sale, then add one to your collection every year.

Hanging basket hell

It happens. Hanging baskets usually look wonderful in stores (especially if they're ready planted), but bring them home and it's hassle city. Baskets require hooks to hang from, they rock in the wind, they dry out quickly, and water drips all over the place.

If you insist on using this type of container,

- ❀ Make absolutely sure the basket is suspended safely (see pages 120–21).
- ❀ Hang the basket above other plants so they can benefit from the excess water dripping out.
- ❀ Don't hang the basket too high. Make sure you can reach it easily for watering.

- Position it where runoff water won't dribble down and soak the people on the balcony below you.
- Avoid wire baskets lined with moss or cocoa fiber, especially in a windy, exposed area. (They need watering constantly.) Plastic pots will stay moist longer. They are also lighter.
- Use mostly trailing plants.
- Make sure the basket is big enough—at least 1 ft./30 cm wide. A small, shallow basket will need constant watering.
- Add hydrogel granules (sold in some garden centers) to the planting mix. They hold several hundred times their weight in water. One teaspoonful is sufficient per hanging basket. Soak the granules before adding to the mix.

Some words about window boxes

They're traditional. The first containers that gardeners used for plants raised off the ground were probably window boxes. But they can pose problems. If you have your heart set on some,

- Hang boxes inside the balcony, not outside, and use solid brackets to support them (see page 121).
- Check that box interiors provide enough room to accommodate plants. Many cheap plastic or wooden window boxes are dinky and useless. A good size is 3 ft./1 m long, 1 ft./30 cm deep, and 1 ft./30 cm wide.
- Wooden boxes often leak. Line them with plastic sheeting or garbage bags, then add pebbles and a bit of peat moss. Put flowers planted in plastic pots on top of the peat moss. The advantage of this setup is that you can keep changing the plants throughout the summer (see page 109).

A barrel of fun

Some of the best containers, if you have sufficient space, are old whiskey or wine barrels cut in half. They hold lots of plants, and because they're deep and roomy, perennials can often winter over in them without problems.

If you want to use a barrel for a miniature water garden, be sure to wash it out thoroughly before adding fish. (They can actually get drunk on that leftover single malt.)

The suitability of barrels for gardening comes with a price tag: they are getting absurdly expensive at garden centers. (After all, it's not as though you're buying a new container. Wine and whiskey makers discard them.) Look for barrels that aren't too dried out. Don't buy them if the bottoms are warped and twisted. Watch too for staves that have shrunk so much the metal hoops encasing the barrels have become loose.

And don't pay exorbitant prices for these fun containers. Shop around for the best buy.

Hot tip

"Ask at the supermarket for empty poultry boxes. They are wide, flat cardboard boxes with low sides. They make great temporary work benches for potting up annuals in spring."
—*Sue Martin, balcony gardener*

Get Growing: It's All in the Bag

Soil isn't found in the sky. Unfortunately. For a balcony or rooftop garden, every ounce of the stuff has to be hauled in. It's the most tedious aspect of creating a garden above ground, but there are some advantages.

People with regular gardens down on street level rarely have perfect soil. In its natural state, dirt is usually either too clayey or too sandy. Clay soil clumps together and bakes as hard as a brick in summertime. With sandy soil, water drains away too fast. Amending both with compost, manure, and peat moss into an ideal "friable loam" is backbreaking work, especially if you're restoring an old, neglected garden. It also means buying digging tools like forks and spades. As well, ordinary garden soil may contain fungal diseases or nasty nuisances like cutworms (which love shearing off stems of tomato plants, right after you've planted them).

By contrast, balcony gardeners can get it right the first time. When everything is grown in containers, providing that magical friable formula is a snap. There are usually no bugs to contend with, either. You simply buy bags of the right growing mix from a garden center or hardware store, pot up, and wait for results.

Note those three crucial words: *right growing mix*. Not "soil." Using ordinary garden soil is a definite no-no (however friable it is). Squeezed into the artificial environment of a pot, plants need more cosseting than Mother Earth can provide. Potted plants can't ramble anywhere they please (as they do in a regular garden), so air spaces must be trapped in their containers to help roots breathe. Also, because the space is unnaturally small, nutrients need to be replenished regularly. Finally, there should be good drainage; plants don't like to sit with wet feet any more than we do. Specially formulated growing mixes are designed to meet those needs.

What do growing mixes contain?

Visit a garden center and there's a bewildering variety of growing mixes to choose from. Labels on the big, shiny bags often make extravagant claims ("Perfect perennials in two weeks!"; "Grow tomatoes as big as baseballs!"), but they're vague and unhelpful about the actual ingredients of the mix.

> **Hot tip**
> "Keep a folding luggage carrier, a big plastic laundry hamper, and a bungee cord in your car. Use for hauling bags of soil upstairs in spring."
> —*Sue Martin, balcony gardener*

Here's why: most of them contain the same thing—lots of peat moss. This natural ingredient, which is harvested from former bogs, is used for container-grown plants because it retains moisture well. However, peat moss doesn't have a lot of nutrients, so most mix makers supplement it with chemical fertilizers in different formulas. They also may add composted softwood bark, vermiculite (which looks like nubbly bits of Styrofoam), or perlite (which is usually also nubbly and is made from heated lava rock). Bentonite clay may be included too, to help retain water.

Because peat moss is the prime ingredient in virtually all mixes, "expensive" doesn't automatically mean "better." It pays to shop around and experiment with different products. A garden writer who conducted some tests found that mixes varied enormously. Some stayed too soggy. One had too much nitrogen (so flowering plants produced lots of leaves but few blooms). Another was so fluffy with vermiculite, water whooshed through containers in seconds and didn't stay long enough to give plants a drink. And in one test, the most costly mix performed the worst.

You'll also see bags labeled "potting soil." Often this is simply soil, but it may have peat moss, compost, sand, and vermiculite added. It can be excellent or poor, depending on the company that packaged it. Again, experiment. Also, remember that bags of potting soil weigh more than mixes made with peat moss, so they may be a bigger hassle to haul upstairs.

The advantage of using ready-made mixes is that they are (usually) sterile. Manufacturers heat them to 180°F/82°C to kill bacteria and weed seeds. However, convenience comes at a price. If you need to fill lots of pots and planters, mixes can get mighty expensive.

Making your own mix

Good cooks work from scratch, rather than using pre-packaged ingredients. So do experienced gardeners, because it's cheaper and they can control what goes into the mix. To do this, spread out a big piece of plastic sheeting on the balcony floor or use a plastic garbage bin. Wear gloves if you don't like to get messy.

Two mixes recommended by condo gardeners

Pauline Walsh suggests: "Buy equal parts of potting soil, peat moss, triple mix (which contains peat moss, soil, and manure), and vermiculite. Keep mixing them till they look nice and crumbly. Once you've filled the pots, sprinkle aquarium charcoal on top. This absorbs odors and helps keep the soil sweet and moist." Her herbs flourish on this formula.

Elsa Young, whose terrace is full of magnificent clematis and roses, makes this recommendation: "Combine a bag each of composted sheep manure, peat moss, and a soil-less mix that contains vermiculite. Add several handfuls of bone meal."

More mix tips

❀ Avoid composted horse manure (unless it's three years old). It's too salty for most plants.

❀ Add a smidgen of horticultural sulphur or aluminum sulfate (sold at garden centers) if you're growing acid-loving plants like rhododendrons.

❀ A scoop of builder's sand is good, especially for herbs and cactus. Buy it at home reno stores and builders' yards. Don't use beach sand, which is too fine.

❀ If you're buying a ready-made mix, add a handful of granular slow-release fertilizer before planting. (It's usually sold in plastic jars or boxes.) First, however, always read what's written on your bag of growing mix. If it says something like, "With special nutrients added," that means fertilizer and you shouldn't add any.

❀ Never be a cheapskate and get soil from a friend's garden. Besides offering inadequate nutrients, soil packs down too hard in containers and may harbor diseases and creepy-crawlies that will multiply like mad in your pots.

What is humus?

If you're puzzled by that funny word "humus," don't be. It simply means decomposed or decayed organic matter. Peat moss is humus. So are composted leaves. It often looks exactly like topsoil. If you see a bag labeled "humus" at the garden center, it may contain some kind of composted material, leaves, or tree bark (or all three.) It's all good stuff.

Fertilizer facts

Gardeners who worry about the environment usually don't like to do anything "artificial." However, the fact is, most container-grown plants need fertilizer. There isn't sufficient nourishment in pots for them to flourish long term without some kind of boost.

If you pot up in spring using a growing mix that has fertilizers included (or some granular stuff that you added yourself), plants will usually do fine for a couple of months. But by mid-summer, they're probably getting tired and have used up the nutrients in the mix. That's the time to start fertilizing. If, however, you've used a mix that contains no additives (they consist of pure peat moss, compost, or potting soil), begin a regime of fertilizing right after planting.

There are many good fertilizers aimed at home gardeners. Often, they are simply called "plant food." Some are crystals, others liquid, and you stir them into a jug of water. Whichever type you use, let the mix sit for a few hours before pouring on plants. (Avoid touching leaves). If you have a garden hose, fertilizer granules that go into a gizmo attached to the hose are even easier. Some gardeners swear by little fertilizer "sticks" that are pushed into the soil. If you use these, be careful not to overdo them, or plant roots may get burned.

Check the numbers

Confused by all those mysterious numbers on the bottle or package of plant food? Here's a brief explanation.

All fertilizers contain these three basic nutrients:

❀ Nitrogen (chemical symbol N) promotes growth of green leaves and stems.

❀ Phosphorus (chemical symbol P) helps roots, flowers, and fruit grow.

❀ Potassium (chemical symbol K) assists flowering and fruiting too, but also makes plants develop strong stems and resistance to disease.

The three symbols are listed as numbers on product labels, always in that order. When you see something that says 5-10-5, it means the product contains 5% nitrogen, 10% phosphorus, and 5% potassium.

What's best to use? It depends on your plants. A good all-round formula is 20-20-20 or 10-10-10. This works well with most houseplants and it's fine for flowers grown out of doors, particularly annuals. Leafy plants prefer a formula where nitrogen is emphasized, for instance 10-7-7.

<table>
<tr><td>Hot tip
"If you're growing annuals and want lots of flowers, try using a fertilizer that's formulated for tomatoes. It really works."
—Ben Ng, window box gardener</td></tr>
</table>

Organic or chemical?

Which is best? Both have merits. So-called natural fertilizers—often composted manure, fish emulsion, bone meal, or blood meal—are more expensive, but take effect slowly and generally won't harm plants. Chemical products get results quicker, but can burn leaves and roots if used incorrectly. Ultimately, the choice is a personal one. Look for a product that suits what you're growing, and follow label instructions to the letter. More plants are killed by people being too generous with fertilizer than by anything else.

When to fertilize?

Most balcony gardeners do it every two weeks. Some swear by a weekly regime. Don't fertilize at all during a heat wave, because it stresses plants. Wait till the weather cools down a bit. Also, stop fertilizing in the fall.

How to plant

Do

✓ Plant in the evening, not during the heat of the day.

✓ Choose a day when rain is forecast. Plants seem to love a good soak right after being planted.

✓ Soak growing mixes thoroughly before filling pots. (If they're in bags, cut the bag open and pour a jug of water in. Let it sit overnight.)

✓ Add granular fertilizer if necessary and be sure to follow the manufacturer's instructions as to quantity.

✓ Fill containers two-thirds full with growing mix.

✓ Arrange plants on top of the mix (still in their little plastic pots, if possible). Keep moving them around until you get an arrangement that satisfies you.

✓ Use plenty of plants. They can be closer together than in a regular garden. Put plants that will grow tall in the center (or at the back of a long planter). Trailing ones are best around the edge.

✓ Loosen root balls with your fingers if they're tightly packed, then push them gently into the mix. (Make sure root balls aren't dried out when you do this. They should be damp.) Push a bit more soil in around the plants with your hands.

✓ Check that you haven't planted the root balls too high. They should not be sticking up above the surface of the mix. If they are, start again.

✓ If plants are already flowering, pinch their flower heads right off. (Yes, off. It may seem crazy, but plants will settle in better and get bushier if you deflower them at the beginning.)

✓ Water deeply, so it comes out the drainage holes.
✓ With large plants (and trees and shrubs), dig a hole in the container that's twice the width of the root ball. Then fill it with water and let it drain away before you plant. A dollop of a new growth supplement called Myke (sold at garden centers) will help them get established. Follow the manufacturer's instructions as to quantity.
✓ If you're growing annuals, add broken up bits of Styrofoam or packing peanuts to the bottom of large containers before putting growing mix in. The containers won't weigh as much, and you'll spend less on growing mix. (But don't do this with big perennials, shrubs, or trees. Their roots need every inch of space they can get in containers.)

Don't

✗ Use dry mix. Peat moss needs to soak up water first. If it's too dry when you plant, it may stay that way forever. Your plants will never receive enough moisture.
✗ Fill pots too full. Leave at least 1 in./2.5 cm of head space so water and soil don't dribble over the top.
✗ Put bits of old pots or crockery in the bottom of the pot. Yes, it's accepted practice, but it's not necessary and it adds to the pot's weight. If you're worried about soil falling out the hole, put a cheap, lightweight sponge or coffee filter in the bottom of the pot.
✗ Pack the soil down hard.
✗ Put pots in direct sunshine right after you've planted them. Keep them in shade for a couple of days to settle in.
✗ Plant anything in really torrid temperatures. Wait for a cooler day.

Hot tip

"Put a piece of self-watering mat, sold at garden centers, in the bottom of your pots. It helps to wick moisture up into the soil."

—Pauline Walsh, balcony gardener

Townhouse troubles

If you're gardening on the ground in a townhouse courtyard, be prepared for extra work. Lots of it. The so-called soil around new townhouse developments is usually little more than construction debris, topped with a thin layer of earth (or sod) to prettify its appearance. Don't be tempted to plant in this miserable stuff; nothing will grow well. The only remedy is to dig everything out and replace it with real topsoil. Mix in some gritty sand, peat moss, and composted sheep manure too, if you intend to grow flowers. It's backbreaking work, but you will be starting off right.

Yes, you can compost

Composting will help the environment and your bank balance. Even on a tiny balcony, it's possible to recycle vegetable scraps—and produce that lovely, dark brown crumbly stuff that plants love. Here's how:

❀ In the fall, empty soil from some of your pots into a big garbage bag. Mix in a small bag of leaves gathered from the street. (Avoid oak leaves, which often take ages to break down, and cut the leaves up a bit, if you can.)

❀ Stand empty pots (which should be at least 15 in./40 cm wide) in an accessible place.

❀ Cut vegetable scraps into tiny pieces, add a bit of water, then keep mixing these scraps in your empty pots with trowelfuls of soil from the garbage bag.

❀ The veggie matter will quickly break down, so long as you keep introducing air to your mini-pile by working it with the trowel. As one pot fills up, put it aside and start on another pot.

❀ Use only plastic or fiberglass containers, because clay will crack during the winter. And don't worry about the stuff freezing. If it does, you can resume mixing once it warms up.

❀ Cover containers with lids if you're worried about flies and pests (though they are seldom a problem).

❀ Add tea bags and coffee grounds to your compost. But leave out the coffee filters. They take too long to break down.

❀ If you're brave enough, add a cupful of your own urine to the mix sometimes. It's full of nitrogen and really helps break things down.

Made-in-a-pot compost is ready to use the following spring when it feels crumbly. (If the texture isn't quite right, add a bit of peat moss.)

Alternatively, on a large balcony or rooftop, there may be room to squeeze in a mini-composter. These are boxy plastic contraptions with lids and aerating slats cut into the sides. Many municipalities give them out free, or at a reduced rate, to gardeners. If you use one, position it in the sun or shade

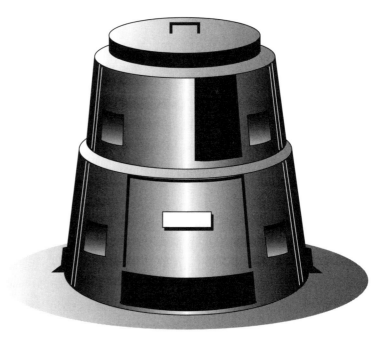

Mini-composter

(either works well) in a spot where the air can circulate freely. Then follow the three basic rules for creating compost quickly: cut everything you put into the composter into small pieces, mix wet and dry in layers, and keep turning the pile.

You don't need more growing mix

In spring, top up all your containers with a scoop of homemade compost. It's cheaper—and easier—than going out and buying fresh bags of mix.

Just Add Water (Often)

One big drawback to growing things in containers is often overlooked: watering. You can't escape it. Relying on the rain won't work. Any plant with its roots cramped into a container will dry out much more quickly than when it's growing in a regular garden. As well, many balcony gardeners are cursed with a concrete overhang, so rainwater can't reach plants.

Balconies, terraces, and rooftops can also be subject to non-stop winds that aren't even noticed on the ground. This dries things out even more. In summertime, your plants will usually need a drink once, sometimes twice, a day. If you neglect them for even twenty-four hours, they may give up the ghost.

Signs that you aren't watering enough include:

- ❀ Leaves shriveled, brown, or dried at edges
- ❀ Entire plant—or parts of it—drooping
- ❀ Flowers or leaves falling off prematurely
- ❀ Soil that's dusty, baked hard as a brick, cracking open, blowing out, or pulling away from the sides of pots

Wise ways to water

Do
✓ Water in the early morning, if you can. It's the best time. But if you have to wait till later, don't worry. That stuff about "wet foliage getting burned by the sun" is exaggerated.
✓ Install an outside faucet, if you can afford it.
✓ Invest in a hose that doesn't take up much space. Some are self-coiling (that is, they have springy tubing, like

telephone cords). Other, more expensive ones flatten out after use, like firefighters' hoses. Check that you can attach such hoses to the kitchen tap.

✓ Fit the hose with a snap-on watering wand. Add the kind of adjustable nozzle that pokes directly into containers. (Avoid a wide "rose" nozzle.)

✓ Water deeply. Make sure the entire soil mass is wet.

✓ Be extra careful to regularly water anything you've just planted. Don't allow it to dry out.

✓ Put dishes (old saucers, pie plates, or made-for-the-job catch basins, sold at garden centers) under containers to catch the water. Raise the pots up a bit, on pebbles or broken bits of old clay pots, so air can circulate.

Don't

✗ Forget to water once the fun of spring planting wears off.

✗ Water late at night. Once in a while is okay, but a regular nocturnal routine is out. Plants that stay damp overnight get mildew and slugs.

✗ Use softened water, if you can avoid it. It's salty, and plants don't like it.

✗ Spray water on leaves, which can cause ugly spotting and fungal diseases. It's best to wet the soil and roots.

✗ Leave water sitting in dishes under pots for longer than a day. Stagnant water is a perfect breeding ground for mosquitoes. It will also stink. (It's not good for plants, either. Their roots may rot.) Tip the water out of small dishes; in bigger ones, suck it out with a turkey baster or mop it up with a sponge.

Try the tepid treatment

Buy a big plastic pail, not a pretty watering can. Keep this pail in an unobtrusive place, and fill it with water every morning. Let it stand for several hours. Then scoop the contents out with an empty yogurt container or plastic jug and pour directly onto soil around plants. This works particularly well because

- ❀ Plants (especially newly potted ones) prefer tepid water.
- ❀ You can direct the water where it matters most.
- ❀ It doesn't wet everything else the way watering cans do.

How to cut down on watering

- ❀ Grow plants in large containers. The bigger the planter, the slower it will dry out.
- ❀ Don't use clay pots. Plastic or resin will hold water longer.
- ❀ Group plants together in spots that aren't windy.
- ❀ Forget hanging baskets. They fry quickly in the heat (especially those lined with moss).
- ❀ Use a growing mix that contains moisture-retaining perlite or vermiculite.
- ❀ Put a piece of landscaping cloth or a folded piece of newspaper in the bottom of pots before adding soil. This will help stop water from draining away too quickly.
- ❀ Put mulch over the tops of all your containers. If you don't have any, use old newspapers, cut to fit.
- ❀ Check labels at garden centers and don't buy anything that says, "Needs a moist location."

How to rescue dried-out plants

Fill the kitchen sink and dunk the entire plant into it. Water should be at least an inch over the top of the container. Leave

Grow things that can survive with little water

Annual flowers include coreopsis, gazanias, morning glories, nasturtiums, portulacas, some types of salvia, and the stubby orange marigold (Tagetes). Among perennials, try sedums, hens and chicks, grasses, yarrows, and tropical plants like echeverias, jade plants, and cacti. Some geraniums (usually the varieties called "ivies") are also drought-tolerant. Check their labels.

immersed until bubbles have stopped coming to the surface. Remove and keep out of the sun for a couple of days.

Pots too big to lift into the sink? Try soaking them thoroughly with a stream of water from a hose for ten minutes (but be careful of the poor souls on the balcony below).

Do you overwater?

Beginners are often guilty of this. If leaves are turning yellow, the stems are soft and transparent-looking, or the soil is sodden all the time, not simply moist, you may be overwatering.

Rescue routine: remove the plant from the pot carefully and let the whole thing dry out, sitting in a dish. Snip off moldy, mushy, or blackened bits of roots. Don't put the dish in sunshine. Place a sheet of newspaper or cloth over the plant so roots aren't exposed to light. Once the soil feels damp but not wet, restore the plant to its pot with fresh growing mix.

When you go on vacation

Group plants together. Move them to the shade, if they're in hot sun. Take hanging baskets off hooks and put them on the balcony floor. Give everything a good soak, then wad damp newspapers over the tops of containers, around the plants.

Then talk nicely to the neighbors. The smartest course of action is to have someone come in to water during your absence. If that's not possible, look into buying an automatic drip irrigation kit. Most require an outside faucet, a timer, and quite a bit of fiddling about with tubing and clamps to set up. They can also leak or clog and must be checked regularly.

You can also make a primitive self-watering system. Fill a bucket of water. Cut some long strands of thick wool or sisal twine. Put one end of the strands into the bucket and the other end into the soil in your containers. This will wick some (but not much) water into the plants.

Getting Started with Plants

Gardening has become the number one pastime of many North Americans. (Surveys consistently put it ahead of sex and watching television.) As a result, growers keep coming out with more and more varieties of plants to seduce us. Nowadays, you can easily go crazy looking at all those little pots with labels at garden centers. It's hard to know which ones to buy—and what to do with them.

Annuals and perennials: What's the difference?

If you've never grown anything before and wonder where to start, here's what you need to know: all garden plants (except shrubs, trees, bulbs, and tropical exotica, which we'll get to later) are classified for home gardeners as "annuals" or "perennials." In a northern climate, you plant annuals every spring, enjoy them for the summer, then ditch them in the fall (preferably on a compost heap) because they won't survive outside during the winter. Perennials are another matter. They can endure cold temperatures and keep coming up year after year. So you plant them once, and leave them to become permanent fixtures in the garden (or in pots and planters on your balcony).

Which are best for a balcony—or other small spaces—where they'll be confined to containers? Annuals and perennials have different attributes. Annuals are mostly easy to grow, and they provide continuous color throughout the summer. Their drawback is that you have to keep potting up new ones every spring. Perennials can be more interesting plants, but they have much shorter blooming periods. They may produce flowers in spring, summer, or fall, but rarely in all three seasons. That means they often take up valuable space in pots and planters when they aren't looking their best. You also have to give perennials special care in the winter (see pages 132–35), which can be a hassle in condos or apartments.

Beginners should try annuals first.

Understanding plant labels

Be sure to read those tags stuck into plant pots. Whether the plants are annuals or perennials, most tags carry symbols that will tell you the growing requirements. In the matter of sun versus shade, plant growers divide their offerings into three basic categories. These are:

○ A completely white circle means the plant needs full sun. This means at least six unobstructed hours of sunshine (with no shade from trees or buildings) every day.

◑ A circle split in two—one half white, the other black—means part sun. At least half a day of sunshine (i.e., three hours) is required. Most plants prefer morning sun. If your unit faces west, you'll need a bit more unobstructed sunshine in the afternoon—a total of, say, four hours —for plants in this category to flourish.

● A solid black circle means the plant prefers no direct sunshine at all. But we're not talking "total darkness" here. Remember that all plants need some light to grow. Just don't put anything with this kind of label where it will get direct sunshine in the heat of the day.

When labels carry two symbols
Confusingly, you'll sometimes see plant labels with two symbols. The tag might indicate "full sun" and "part sun." Or it says "part sun" and "shade."

What this means is the plant can grow in a range of conditions. It may prefer full sun, but will cope with some shade. Or it's a shade-loving plant, but it doesn't mind some sun.

What is "dappled shade"?

Once upon a time, poets waxed eloquent about "dappled" mares. They were talking about horses, of course, but now the horticultural world has taken over the term. In gardening books and catalogues, "dappled" means shade from surrounding trees. Buildings cast solid shade (the sun obviously can't penetrate through concrete), but with foliage, the shadows are less fixed. Some light filters through, particularly on a windy day, when leaves sway to and fro. That's dappled shade. Plants that carry tags with "part sun" or "part shade" circles are the kind to buy if your growing space gets this kind of light.

Know your hardiness zone

Experienced gardeners are fond of tossing around strange expressions like, "Ah, Zone 6," in reference to plants. This can be bewildering for beginners. Here are a few words of explanation.

All the regions of North America are divided up into hardiness zones for the purposes of agriculture and horticulture. The main factor in delineating these zones is how low the temperature dips in winter (because that determines whether or not a plant will survive until next spring). The warmer the weather, the higher the hardiness zone number. For example, Zone 1 is way up—brr—in the Arctic tundra. But by the time you travel south to Zone 11, you're down Mexico way.

It's important to know what hardiness zone you live in. Many beginner gardeners don't bother to find this out—and they wind up wasting a lot of money on expensive perennials, shrubs, and trees that promptly bite the dust once winter comes. Maps of hardiness zones are often published in gardening books. Examine them, but don't trust the information (frequently presented in a complex chart) implicitly. For clarification, ask at a local garden center, because various climatic influences in your area can skew your hardiness zone. The books may state that you live in Zone 5, but they won't take into account a local body of water, or the fact that you garden high off the ground, on a windy, exposed balcony. These kinds of factors can ratchet your zone up—or down—a notch or two.

Once you know your hardiness zone, always check that the plants you're buying match it. Don't try to overwinter a Zone 7 plant if you garden in Zone 5. It will almost certainly die. There is a lot of blather nowadays about "zonal denial"—that is, ignoring hardiness zones, planting what you please, and keeping your fingers crossed. While this can be fun, it's not recommended for people who grow things in containers, particularly on balconies or rooftops. Plants have a hard enough time surviving off the ground; we don't need to stress them any further.

Look on plant tags. Sometimes the hardiness zones are listed, but often they aren't. If in doubt, ask the garden center staff—and don't be fobbed off by some summer employee who isn't sure. Ask to see the horticulturist. This is crucial information. Make sure you get it before forking over your hard-earned cash for plants—particularly perennials, shrubs, and trees.

Ask your neighbors
They probably know better than anybody else what plants will work—and which ones to avoid. Before blowing a bundle of bucks at a garden center, get their input.

Moving houseplants outside: Is it wise?

Yes, but with caution. Houseplants are like people who live in northern climates heading south for winter vacations. Both need time to acclimatize to new surroundings. If you suddenly plunk plants outside on a hot, sunny balcony when they've been accustomed to life indoors, they may get as sunburned as we do on a beach in the Bahamas. However, unlike humans, plants may never recover from the shock.

Light levels inside our homes are invariably lower than out of doors. (This applies even if you have plants on sunny window ledges or under lights.) So it pays to break prized specimens into their summer environment slowly.

Some gardeners prefer not to move their indoor plants outside at all. They insist that doing so weakens the plants and that they are better off staying in the same environment year-round. Other gardeners disagree. They find that, like humans, plants benefit from a dollop of the fresh air and sunshine after being cooped up indoors over the winter. The choice is yours. If you do decide to haul houseplants out onto your balcony or rooftop,

Do

✓ Put all houseplants (grouped together for protection) in a shady corner of your balcony that doesn't receive *any* direct sunlight for at least a couple of weeks.

✓ If the indirect light is fierce, gently cover the plants with an old sheet for the first week. Water really well.

✓ Keep the kind of houseplants that normally thrive in low-light conditions—philodendrons, Chinese evergreens, and spider plants—in shade all summer.

✓ Bring cacti, rosemary bushes, bay trees, amaryllis, and
  succulents like jade plants into the sun after an adjustment
  period. Give them only an hour of sunshine at first, then
  gradually increase it. (Grouping them on a trolley with
  castors is a good idea, if you have space.)
✓ Prune houseplants back at the end of summer. Then give
  them a bath before they come indoors again (see page 133).

Don't

✗ Subject plants to "reverse shock" in fall. It's foolish to
  leave things outside until the temperature plummets, then
  expect them to adjust instantly to hot, dry central heating.
  As in spring, plants need to acclimatize slowly.
✗ Immediately toss a plant out that got nipped by frost. It
  may be salvageable. Cut all the foliage off, water well, and
  wait to see if new shoots appear.

Exciting Annuals, New and Old

Out of fashion for years, annuals are back big time. There is, in fact, an extraordinary variety of single-season flowers and foliage plants available now. In warmer climates, it's possible to treat some of the following as perennials. But if you're a northern gardener, just enjoy their burst of glory for one summer.

How to buy annuals

Do

✓ Buy pre-started plants, in little cell paks. You usually get four or six small plants to a pak.

✓ Check out greengrocers and corner stores in your city neighborhood. They often have great selections of plants.

✓ Ask storeowners what works well locally. They're often very knowledgeable (and are frequently far more interested in helping you than summer students at garden centers).

✓ Buy early in the season, when there's more to choose from and plants are fresh.

✓ Choose small plants with lots of bud tips. They'll settle in better than those with stems and flower heads already shooting up everywhere.

✓ Check the undersides of cell paks. If a mess of roots is sticking out the bottom, the plants have been potted too long and may not be worth buying.

✓ After planting, pinch out the main flower buds on pre-started plants. This may sound crazy, but it will promote bushy growth.

Don't

✗ Buy anything that has yellowing leaves, is long and leggy, or is completely dried out.

✗ Trust all the labels. Shoppers often switch them!

✗ Leave plants sitting in cell paks too long. If you can't plant right away, be sure to keep them in a shady spot and slosh some water over them.

✗ Start annuals from seed (except nasturtiums). It takes too long.

Four foolproof flowers

In sun, the two Ps: Pansies and petunias

Pansies and petunias are a cinch in pots and window boxes. Both come in wonderful colors, and they always make a great show.

Pansies are cute little flowers with "faces" (which everybody loves) and are usually trouble-free. Plant them close together in pots as soon as the weather starts to warm up (if there's still frost, wait), but remember too that pansies are primarily cool-weather flowers. They can't take searing heat and will tolerate some shade. Most varieties are finished by July (unless you water constantly), and then you'll probably have to replace them with something else. Don't bother with the much ballyhooed Icicle pansies. While they are frost-tolerant, they are primarily of interest to people who plant pansies in ground-level flowerbeds and want them to stay there year-round. Some good pansy combinations:

❀ For pizzazz: three bright varieties, like purple, yellow, and orange

❀ For trendy Wendys: black and white

❀ For lovers of Provence: cobalt blue pansies (sans faces), on their own or with yellow

> ## Hot tip
> "Don't buy pre-started pansies with big, juicy leaves. You'll get more flowers if the leaves are smaller."
>
> —Jennifer Reynolds, gardening editor

- For old-fashioned elegance: luscious antique shades—apricots, creams, salmon, and orange. These are hard to find nowadays because they take longer to germinate than other varieties, so growers don't bother with them. Grab heirloom varieties if you can.

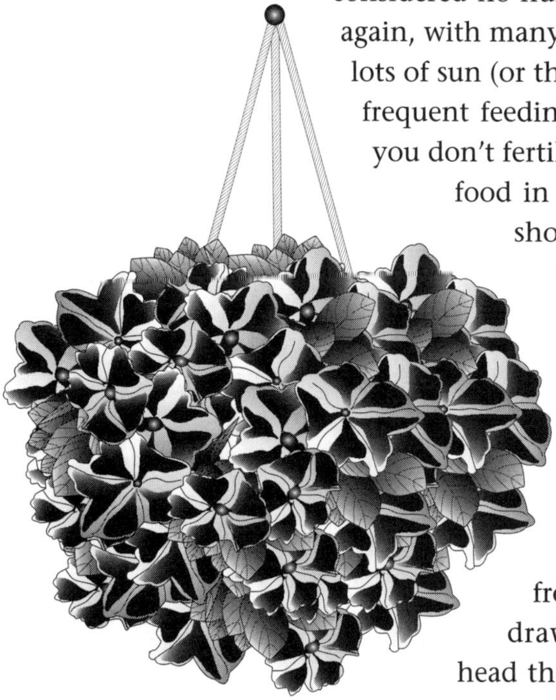

Petunias have been around for donkey's years and were considered ho-hum for a while. But now they are hot again, with many yummy shades and sizes. They need lots of sun (or they get straggly, with few flowers) and frequent feeding. They will die down in summer if you don't fertilize weekly (with a water-soluble plant food in a formula like 14-14-14). Most have showy, single blooms, but look for pretty doubles and coin-sized minis too. New Surfinia and Wave varieties and Balcon minis develop into wonderful, cascading mats of flowers that are great for window boxes and planters. A look-alike flowering annual called Calibrachoa Million Bells also works well. Wait till all frosts are finished before planting. One drawback to petunias: you must deadhead them or they won't continue to flower all summer, and most varieties feel horribly sticky. Keep gardening gloves handy! Some great petunia pairings:

- Two pink varieties: shocking pink with pale pink (but don't use against red brick walls)
- White with beet red or purple
- Scarlet with cream (beautiful against brick)
- Pink or red petunias with bidens (*Bidens ferulifolia*) and licorice vine (*Helichrysum petiolare*) in either silver or the yellow-green Limelight variety (but watch this vigorous vine: its roots may get too pushy in a pot and suffocate the petunias)
- Golden yellow *Calibrachoa* Million Bells, which comes in both upright and trailing varieties, with trailing purple lobelia

For shade, the two Cs: Coleus and caladiums

Coleus and caladiums are foliage plants, which means their leaves are the alluring part. While plants without blooms may sound boring to beginners, coleus and caladiums look as dazzling as any flower, particularly up against concrete. Their big asset? They won't sulk in shade.

Coleus is originally from Malaysia and has a correct name that's a real tongue twister: *Solenostemon scutellarioides*. It is treated as an annual in northern climates, and it's a snap to

grow. Victorians went nuts over its flamboyant foliage, but then it careened into oblivion (dismissed as "too garish"). Now it's back with a vengeance: there are dozens of varieties, with fun names like Cranberry Salad and Inky Fingers. Look for the Avalanche series, which comes in truly riotous colors. Coleus produce a nondescript spike of pale blue flowers. Some people pinch this off (because it detracts from the leaves), but lazy gardeners can ignore it.

Coleus tips:

- ❀ Perk up a dark corner with scarlet, magenta, and bronze varieties planted together.
- ❀ Purple- or maroon-leaved coleus look good with any pink, orange, or white flowers. (Begonias are a good bet if you have a shady balcony.)
- ❀ Mix green and yellow coleus varieties with something scarlet, like geraniums (in sun).

⚜ Use the colors of coleus to "echo" the shades of other plants. For instance, combine a golden coleus that has red streaks with a scarlet monkey flower (*Mimulus* x *hybridus*).

Caladiums are from South America and are not as hassle-free as coleus. Keen gardeners with lots of space buy them as tubers in early spring and start them indoors. For a balcony, simply buy ready-potted caladiums. They have gorgeous, heart-shaped leaves, often as delicate as tissue paper, which unfurl like flags. Colors are striking pinks, reds, and greens, or white with veining in green and red. Their flower spikes should be cut off (they suck energy from the leaves). You can bring caladiums indoors for the winter, but they tend to be temperamental. It's easier to buy new ones every spring. How to use them:

⚜ Combine caladiums with spiky houseplants (like *dracaena*) brought outdoors for the summer.
⚜ Pair white varieties with brightly colored coleus in shady corners.
⚜ Position next to a pond (they like it damp).

Twenty-five great annuals

⚜ **Allysum:** Sold at just about every garden center. Considered ho-hum by hoity horts, but the white or mauve mats of flowers are a great edger in front of other plants. Easy. Needs sun to produce lots of flowers. Shear back after flowering and it will bloom again.
⚜ **Bacopa (*Sutera cordata*):** Pretty little white flowers, with dark green leaves. Good if you have shade because it tends to wilt in full sun. Water regularly. There's also a lavender variety called Pink Domino or Mauve Mist.
⚜ **Bells of Ireland (*Moluccella laevis*):** A novelty plant. In late summer, it produces stems of green "bells," in

which tiny white or pink flowers nestle. The bells turn white and papery and are great for fall floral arrangements.

❀ **Bidens** (pronounced bye-denz): A European annual, now hot with gardeners everywhere. Produces pretty small trailing flowers in yellow, with bright green foliage. Try it with scarlet geraniums. Bidens takes time to get established, but is otherwise easy and drought-tolerant. It self-seeds everywhere, but you can yank out the "volunteers."

❀ **Blue fan flower (*Scaevola aemula*):** Another trendy trailer. Blooms are an interesting shape (they fan sideways), and the divine blue-violet color goes well with anything.

❀ **Brachyscome:** Also known as the Swan River daisy. Flowers come in a variety of colors: white, pink, yellow, purple. Good mixed with trailing plants. It grows about 1 ft./30 cm tall and needs sun.

❀ **Browallia:** A garden stalwart with star-shaped blue or white flowers that grows to about 1 ft./30 cm and does well in semi-shade. Looks good with any other annual.

❀ **Cosmos:** Cheap and cheerful, mostly with white, pink, or magenta flowers and pretty feathery foliage. Try the offbeat Sea Shells, with peculiar pink petals rolled into tubes. Most cosmos are tall and floppy (put them behind something shorter), but the dwarf Klondike series reaches only 1 ft./30 cm high and is great in containers. They need sun. Deadhead regularly.

❀ **Fuchsias:** For balconies without much direct sun. Most have flowers that droop downwards. Best in hanging baskets or raised containers where you can see blooms up close, because their shapes are fascinating. Some look like frilly skirts on ballet dancers.

❀ **Gazanias:** Zingy yellow, red, or orange daisy-like flowers offset by grey-green foliage. Truly drought-tolerant. (Forget to water and gazanias don't give up.) Needs full sun and heat to flourish. One drawback: flowers on some varieties stay closed on cloudy days. Look for the less reclusive

Daybreak kind. The compact Chansonette blooms earlier than the rest.

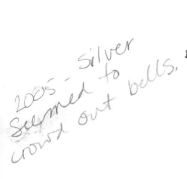

Try in 2007?

2005 - silver seemed to crowd out bells.

❀ **Heliotrope:** Out of style for years, now back. Purple flowers and nice green foliage. Its smell is supposed to be like cherry pie, but that's debatable. Will grow in semi-shade; don't let it dry out. Combine with any flower in white, pink, or magenta, and green-leaved trailers like licorice vine and Plectranthus.

❀ **Lantana:** A tropical plant that grows into a big, beautiful bush in the Bahamas. Less pushy in containers in northern climates. Interesting multicolored flowers in yellow, orange, and red. Will bloom all summer if you deadhead it diligently. Needs sun.

❀ **Licorice vine (*Helichrysum petiolare*):** A hot container item because its trailing leaves—like silver velvet—harmonize with anything. Try the Limelight variety too. Its yellow-green leaves are a knockout with scarlet. Be careful, though: this is a pushy plant that loves squeezing out the competition. A thin-leaved variety, Spike, is less likely to suffocate other plants.

❀ **Lobelia:** Another garden mainstay, with small flowers in an intense blue or purple. Backs up flowers of any color well. Prefers cool weather. In torrid temperatures, lobelia will languish. Shear it back; it'll bloom again. The Cascade kind is a trailing plant, best for containers. Tolerates some shade.

❀ **Monkey flower (*Mimulus* x *hybridus*):** Bright orange, red, or yellow flowers with funny purple spots. Definitely an acquired taste. Pair with a leafy plant in dark green. Likes lots of water.

❀ **Morning glories (*Ipomoea*):** Climbers with spectacular but short-lived flowers, long a garden mainstay. What's hot nowadays are two variations: *I. alba* (moonflower vine), with heart-shaped leaves and white flowers that smell gorgeous at night, and *I. batatas* (sweet potato vine), a non-climbing variety grown for its foliage. The latter comes in vivid yellow-green (called Terrace Lime)

Hot tip

"Don't bother to drive out to garden centers in the suburbs if you live in a city neighborhood. I buy all my annuals at local greengrocers and convenience stores."

—*Athina Smardenka, window box gardener*

or deep purple (called Blackie). Both look sensational with most flowers. While regular morning glories need sun, sweet potato vine prefers some shade and will wilt in hot sunshine or wind.

- ❀ **Nasturtium (*Tropaeolum majus*):** Easy-to-grow trailing mainstays, with orange, red, and creamy-colored flowers and juicy green leaves. Avoid the types with variegated foliage (it looks like a viral disease). Nasturtiums prefer poor soil. If the growing mix is nitrogen-rich, you'll get lots of leaves but few flowers. Difficult to transplant. Works best from seed. Plant seeds right after frosts are over, or blooms won't appear till late summer. The flowers and big seedpods taste good. (Sort of peppery. Gourmet chefs love them.)

- ❀ **Nicotiana:** Flowering tobacco. Small varieties, called Nickis, sold everywhere, produce prolific flowers in red, pink, or white and grow about 1 ft./30 cm tall. Mix with trailing plants. Sometimes they are faintly scented, but only true wild tobacco, *N. sylvestris*, has the magical evening fragrance that many gardeners go gaga over. Not for small spaces, *N. sylvestris* grows over 6 ft./2 m tall, with white flower clusters and enormous leaves. Pre-started plants are scarce at garden centers (even though it's easy to grow from seed). In a container, it will send up only one flower spike. Position it in sniffing range. All nicotianas prefer sun (but cope well with part shade) and are prone to attacks by aphids.

[handwritten note: sylvestris Avail @ Vales in 2006]

- ❀ **Oxalis:** Looks like shamrock and is often called the "good luck plant." The purple variety *O. triangularis* has dainty lavender-pink flowers. Does well in sun or shade.

- ❀ **Pentas:** A pretty import from Africa, becoming big as a container plant. Produces clumps of dainty flowers in lavender, pink, or red. Grow in full sun. It can be bothered by aphids. In warmer regions, pentas can be wintered over outside.

- ❀ **Plectranthus:** Mostly trailing plants, often with fuzzy foliage. Related to coleus, they are great for containers, because—like coleus—they grow quickly and combine well with flowers. One popular variety is Mintleaf

(*P. madagascariensis*), which is green edged with white. Keep moist. They don't mind a bit of shade.

❀ **Portulaca:** Out of fashion for years, but hot again—and perfect for containers. For dry, sunny spots. Pretty rose-like flowers in red, orange, yellow, purple, pink, or white, with spiky foliage. Dries out easily. Likes a bit of sand in the growing mix. Look for the Sundial and Sundance varieties, which don't stay closed on cloudy days.

❀ **Snapdragons (*Antirrhinum*):** Available everywhere, easy to grow, many colors. Dwarf varieties are great, but try the Rocket series at the back of a tall planter. Black Prince, with rich red flowers and purple foliage, is lovely (mix it with yellow and violet flowers and gray foliage plants). One plus: you can plant snaps early (they don't mind cool weather) and they keep on blooming till the fall.

❀ **Wishbone flower (*Torenia*):** From Africa and Asia, unknown till a few years ago. Good in semi-shade. Snapdragon-like flowers in white, with pink, blue, and mauve markings. The Clown multicolored varieties are delightful.

❀ **Zinnia:** Pooh-poohed for years by hoity horts, now hot. Produces daisy-like flowers in sunny yellows, oranges, or reds. Its layered petals feel papery when they age. The dwarf Thumbelina series is good in small pots, but tall *Elegans* zinnias will give zip to bigger planters. Needs full sun.

A few to avoid

❀ **Ageratum:** Produces pretty, tufty flowers in violet, pink, purple, or blue, but dries out at the drop of a hat. Then the tufts turn brown and ugly.

❀ **Diascia:** A trendy, unusual plant with pretty little pink flowers. Does best in early spring, but doesn't like wet soil. Tends to turn temperamental in summer. There are both annual and perennial kinds.

- **Osteospermum:** Funny name, fashionable flower, like an exotic daisy. A fave of gardening gurus, but often hard to grow. It dries out too quickly and needs constant dead-heading to flower.

good in 2005

- **Verbena:** Vibrant flowers, sold everywhere, but without full sun and excellent air circulation, all varieties invariably get mildew. *V. bonariensis,* an import from Brazil, is one of the hottest annuals around, sporting gray-green spiky stems topped by tufty violet flowers. Undeniably charming, it grows up to 4 ft./1.5 m high. Try only if you have space and a sheltered but well-ventilated location.

good sometimes — simetime get mildew)

Forget this popular plant

Don't buy impatiens, also known as "busy Lizzie," for pots on balconies. Its flowers and leaves drop everywhere and make a dreadful mess. They will stain wood and concrete. Everyone loves impatiens because they're cheap, tough, and easy to grow, but these flowers are best planted in regular flowerbeds, on the ground.

Perennials:
A Pleasure, but Picky Too

Ask most gardeners what they prefer to grow nowadays and they'll probably say perennials. This category of plants has never been more popular —and it's hardly surprising. There are so many wonderful perennials to choose from. With careful planning, you can have different flowers from spring to fall, coupled with all kinds of perennial foliage plants. And the big plus of this category of plants is that they'll perform all over again next year. There's no need to plant every spring (as you do with annuals).

However, perennials aren't all as trouble-free as garden centers often claim. They also present special problems to people who garden on balconies (or other small spaces). If you want to grow perennials, be aware that

❀ Most perennial flowers have brief blooming periods, lasting a few weeks at most (unlike annuals, which bloom all summer). When they're not in bloom, the foliage of these flowers may look pretty blah on your balcony.

❀ Squeezed into containers, some perennials sulk. Others grow so vigorously they'll need constant dividing. You'll have to keep taking them out of their pots, whacking the root balls in half, and repotting.

❀ Many perennials are not hardy enough to stay unprotected in their containers, above the ground, all winter. If you live in a northern climate, this will mean going through the rigma-role every fall of either wrapping containers in some kind of insulation or hauling them indoors (see pages 132–35).

How to use perennials

Do

✓ Combine perennials and annuals together in containers. That way, you get a colorful show all summer. You'll get the knack of making these combinations as you go along.

✓ Plant perennials in the same growing mix as annuals. Add a slow-release granular fertilizer to the mix. A teaspoon of a new growth supplement called Myke, put into the bottom of each container, will get them off to a good start (but don't overdo it).

✓ Contrary to advice from many experts, try plants that are labeled "invasive." They're often tougher than other perennials and can survive better in containers.

✓ Pot your purchases quickly, especially if you've bought bare-root perennials. Never let them dry out. If you can't plant right away, cover them with sheets of damp newspaper, put them in a shady spot, and sprinkle water on the paper daily.

✓ Tease out roots with a small tool or your hands before planting. If roots are tightly bound together, cut into them with a knife.

✓ Plant perennials more densely in containers than in a regular garden.

✓ Look for "dwarf" and "compact" varieties of perennials. Always ask if a perennial that interests you is suitable for growing in a container (but expect blank looks from many garden center staff).

Don't

✗ Ignore plant labels. It's a waste of time to put a perennial that "needs a moist location" on a hot, dry balcony.

✗ Pick too many perennials at once. Experiment with them a couple at a time.

✗ Add any plant food to the watering can for the first two weeks. Let perennials settle in.

✗ Be discouraged if perennials die. There are plenty more to experiment with.

✗ Grow perennials from seed. It takes too long in containers.

Try these in containers

In sun

❀ **Catmint (*Nepeta*):** Also called catnip. Many kinds. Cats like munching and rolling on some varieties. *N. subsessilis* forms clumps, with pretty fetching upright blue flowers. Good at the front of containers.

❀ **Creeping phlox (*P. subulata*):** In flowerbeds, this multiplies into immense mats a yard across. Containers keep it under control. The mini-mats of little green leaves drape nicely over the edge of pots (mix them with a weeping sedum) and produce little mauve flowers in spring. If it becomes too much of a good thing, it's easy to pull out.

❀ **Daylilies (*Hemerocallis*):** Smaller varieties like Stella D'Oro and a mini relative, Stella D'Oro Lemon Drops, are best in containers. Both keep cranking out golden blooms, which last only a day, well into the fall. If you have a roomy planter, try a daylily that landscapers love, Bonanza. It's tough as old boots. Has limey yellow blooms, blotched with purple. For fragrance, plant lemon yellow *Hemerocallis citrina* (but watch out: it multiplies like crazy). Don't even think of trying daylilies if you have any shade.

❀ **Donkey tail spurge (*Euphorbia myrsinites*):** A curiosity plant, this looks tropical, with funny twirly stems and blue-green leaves, topped by little acid yellow leafy bits in spring. Combines well with other things and doesn't mind dryness. Easy to grow.

❀ **Feverfew (*Tanacetum parthenium*):** This herb, often used to ease headaches, tends to be too much of a good thing in regular gardens, but in containers it's cheery and easy to grow. Has small daisy-like flowers and lovely bright green foliage. Varieties called Golden Moss and Aureum have goldish green leaves.

❀ **Fountain grass (*Pennisetum setaceum*):** Many gardeners can't get enough of ornamental grasses. This one, a beauty, is a perennial in southern climates. In the

Hot tip

"If your perennials are getting too cramped, scoop some soil out of their containers in spring. Then, with an old bread knife, hack a section of the roots off. Remove those bits and top up with new potting soil, mixed with blood meal or bone meal."
—*Sue Martin, balcony gardener*

ELEGANCE PERSONIFIED: Statues make great focal points, even in small spaces. Position them before adding containers and plants. A trellis helps to create privacy.

CAPTIVATING COMBOS:
Pink and white geranium
Freckles (foreground)
harmonizes nicely with
plain pink Horizon, blue
pimpernel (Anagallis)
and (rear right) an
echeveria and magenta
mini petunias.

INEXPENSIVE
ELEGANCE: Four
varieties of coleus and
Tradescantia flumensis
in a plastic urn.

IMPACT STATEMENT:
Don't be afraid to mass
containers in big groups.
The glorious display in
this ground-floor court-
yard includes geraniums,
herbs, succulents and
several shrubs.

*PLANT PROGRESS
(left): A tiny city balcony
is dense with glorious
greenery; Above:
How the same space
looked before the
perennials and
Clematis fargessioides
(top left) filled out.*

*TALL TREAT: Weeping 'Red Jade' crabapple (right), underplanted with licorice vine (*Helichrysum
petiolare*), takes well to containers. Behind the chair, ornamental bunch grass (*Calamagrostis acutiflora
'Karl Foerster') and white* Aster novi-belgii 'Kristina'.

CLIMBING CAVALCADE: Vines like purple Clematis jackmanii *and pink-flowered* Mandevilla *(right) need deep, roomy pots. Grow them up obelisks if you have nowhere to hang a trellis.*

SHELVE IT: Show off ornaments and fave plants on simple wooden shelves attached to fence dividers.

GREEN GROUPING (left): On dry, sunny rooftops, position plants close together to conserve moisture; PLANTER PIZAZZ (below): Scarlet geraniums, shocking pink petunias, blue fan flower, marigolds, trailing euonymus and cascading Calibrachoa Million Bells.

ANNUAL ELEGANCE: Three varieties of geraniums intermingle with white bacopa and yellow dwarf snapdragons.

GLORIOUS GRASSES (above): Two tall varieties,
Miscanthus sinensis 'Silberfeder' (rear left) and
Calamagrostis acutiflora 'Karl Foerster', with blue
grama grass (Bouteloua gracilis, front right), need
sunny locations like this rooftop to flourish; COMING
UP ROSES (above right): Hardy Explorer varieties of
shrub roses, developed in Canada, adapt well to
sky-high conditions. But wrap their containers
in winter.

TURN TO URNS: When fall
comes, ornamental kales
and cabbages, combined with
trailing vinca, are a great
easy-care pick-me-up.

Clockwise from top: SERENE GREEN BACKDROP: Shrubs, ornamental grasses and columnar cedars set off (from left) Stella d'Oro daylilies, spiky white Yucca filamentosa, a red and yellow croton and violet-pink torches of Liatris spicata; WINDOW BOX WOW: Pansies, scarlet geraniums, white and red impatiens, calla lily leaves, and trailing licorice vine are colorful and easy to grow; COOK'S DELIGHT: Tight groups of herbs suit small sunny spaces. Counter-clockwise from left: oregano, chives, mint, bush basil, bay. Behind the cherub, patio rose Red Cascade.

*KNOCK-OUT COLOR: Three Cs—caladiums (foreground), different kinds of coleus, and tall burgundy-leafed cannas (rear)—give a big bang for the buck, as do nasturtiums (center); PASTEL PERFECTION (inset): Lavender spikes with rock daisies (*Brachysome multifida*), yellow* Lysimachia congestifolia, *trailing mintleaf (*Plectranthus madagascariensis*) and a leafy azalea.*

north, treat it as an annual (though it can sometimes be wintered over). It produces purplish fuzzy plumes, with lovely spiky leaves in purple and brownish green that look super with other plants. Grows about 2 ft./60 cm high. If you have a sheltered location and plenty of space, try taller grasses like maiden grass *Miscanthus Gracillimus* 'Silberfeder'—also sometimes called 'Silver Feather'. It grows 8 ft./2.5 m tall, with gorgeous silvery seedheads in fall, and winters over well on rooftops. But remember that all ornamental grasses need *lots* of sun.

❀ **Gardener's garters (*Phalaris arundinacea v. picta*):** Don't plant this terror (also called ribbon grass) in a courtyard flowerbed. It will take over. But the stripy green leaves can be kept under control in containers—and they look great with most flowers. Plant it in front of something tall, like annual cosmos.

❀ **Gayfeathers (*Liatris spicata*):** Fun flowers, with bottle-brush blooms in (usually) a pale purple. Terrific in containers. Their shape contrasts well with rounded flowers, like cosmos or daisies, and with ornamental grasses.

❀ **Phormiums*:*** Tropical foliage plants with big strappy leaves in exciting colors. Very fashionable. Their bold shapes look great in containers, but one drawback is that they must be brought indoors in the fall. A relative, the striking Adam's Needle (*Yucca filamentosa*) is tougher: it can sometimes be wintered over on a balcony.

❀ **Purple coneflowers (*Echinacea purpurea*):** Misnamed (they're pink, not purple), these are like droopy daisies: petals hang downwards from a big, beehive-like seedpod. No matter. They're pretty and easy to grow. Said to be drought-tolerant, but they wilt in dry spells. There's also a white variety.

❀ **Shasta daisies (*Leucanthemum superbum*):** Everybody loves these flowers, but some kinds are too tall and bossy in containers. Try the dwarf Silberprinzesschen, which grows 1 ft./30 cm high, with dainty white flowers. Pinch back in spring, and deadhead flowers.

❀ **Tickseed (*Coreopsis verticillata*):** Frilly little flowers in hot chrome that look great with annuals. A variety

2006

called Moonbeam is fashionable: it has soft, butter yellow blooms. Tends to sprawl. Plant at the back of containers. The common name "tickseed" is rarely used.

Part sun

❀ **Bethlehem sage (*Pulmonaria saccharata*):** One of the first perennials to bloom in spring. Always a delight, it somehow performs the feat of producing pink, violet, and pale blue flowers all on the same stem. The green foliage with white spots looks good too, when flowers have finished. Easy, grows about 1 ft./30 cm high. If leaves get ratty-looking, cut them off; more will quickly appear.

❀ **Cranesbills, or hardy geraniums:** True geraniums (not to be confused with window box geraniums, which are really pelargoniums. See pages 68–71). Dozens of varieties, mostly with tiny flowers. Will tolerate complete shade but you'll get more blooms with a bit of sun. Try Max Frei (*G. sanguineum*), which forms mounds, with bright magenta flowers, and dwarf *G. cinereum,* with gray-green leaves and white or pale pink blooms. Steer clear of Johnson's Blue. Its flowers are a divine color, but the plant gets straggly and messy.

❀ **Heuchera***:* A few years ago, you could only get one variety, with little red flowers and nondescript leaves, called Coral Bells. Now heuchera are so hot a new kind appears every few months. They have metamorphosed into foliage plants, in all shapes and colors, to combine with other plants. Particularly pretty are Palace Pier, Pewter Veil, and Chocolate Ruffles.

❀ **Stonecrop (*Sedum*):** The plant-naming people insisted on saddling this huge family of plants with the monstrous new moniker *Hylotelephiums* a few years ago. Yikes. Fortunately, everyone still calls them sedums. The most forgiving plants on the planet, they tolerate dryness, shade (though they love sun), and all kinds of abuse. Try Gold Moss stonecrop (*S. acre*), which grows only 2 in./5 cm tall, with little yellow flowers. Another dinky variety is *S. spurium*, with fuzzy pinkish blooms. Autumn Joy grows 2 ft./60 cm tall, with bright pink clumpy flowers in late summer; and Vera Jamieson, another tall variety, has oh-so-elegant purply pink leaves.

Shade

❀ **Ferns:** So many to choose from. Go for varieties that won't get too big for their boots. Try shield fern (*Polystichum aculeatum*), which stays reliably evergreen; maidenhair fern (*Adiantum*), which has gorgeous delicate foliage; and Japanese painted fern (*Athyrium nipponicum* 'Pictum'), which is silver-gray and purple. The last one tends to self-seed in gardens, but usually isn't a problem in containers.

❀ **Hostas:** Another fave foliage plant. Many small varieties that suit containers are being introduced. Look for Stiletto and Bitsy Green. They have narrow leaves and won't hog too much space. If you're bothered by creepy-crawlies, there are also slug-resistant hostas (see page 124). Although touted as a shade plant, hostas do fine in sun too (but their layers of leaves spread like mad). In a very shady court-yard, a bed of hostas looks terrific.

❀ **Lady's mantle** (*Alchemilla mollis*): Fascinating leaves, which collect the dew and open like little umbrellas. Grown primarily for its foliage. Produces fuzzy yellow flowers in late spring that can get messy. Often invasive. You may need to divide it after a year or two. Easy to grow.

Hosta

Pick small perennials

Big isn't necessarily a good thing when you're shopping for plants. Small perennials often settle in better than bigger ones, because they go through less transplant shock. What matters more is that plants are healthy-looking, with fresh shoots.

The Joy of Geraniums

Hoity horts hate geraniums, because they're so universally popular and they have brash colors. Ignore the snobs. Geraniums enjoy a justifiably deserved reputation as the "classic window box flower." Europeans have adored their blobs of brightness for centuries. Visit villages in Germany, Greece, and Italy in summertime and they overflow with eye-popping displays of geraniums, mostly in containers. These icons of summer are, in fact, perfect choices for pots and planters, because they provide plenty of oomph without hogging too much space.

Geraniums can be mighty confusing, however. As any gardener in the know will take delight in telling you, the flowers we know as "geraniums" aren't really geraniums at all. Their true name is pelargoniums. You can blame the seventeenth-century botanist Linnaeus for the blooper. He lumped true geraniums—which are perennial plants with small, inconspicuous blossoms (see page 66)—in with their brash tropical cousins. Both belong to the big *Geraniaceae* family, but they're actually different species of plants.

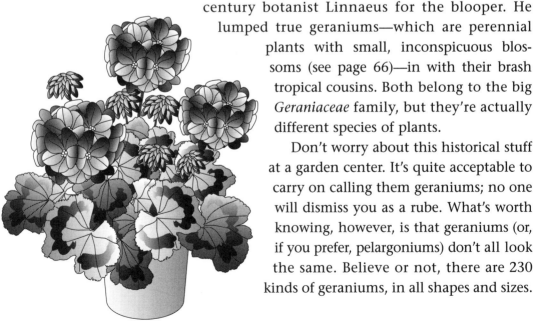

Don't worry about this historical stuff at a garden center. It's quite acceptable to carry on calling them geraniums; no one will dismiss you as a rube. What's worth knowing, however, is that geraniums (or, if you prefer, pelargoniums) don't all look the same. Believe or not, there are 230 kinds of geraniums, in all shapes and sizes.

Types of geraniums

Here are the five kinds you'll see in garden centers most often:

❀ **Zonals:** Traditional geraniums. Easiest to grow. Big show-off blooms, often double. Rounded leaves, frilly at the edges. They reach up to 2 ft./60 cm high. Also called Uprights because of their straight stems. They look good in either a window box or flowerpot, with trailing annuals around their bases. Once, these flowers were used in a tedious triumvirate: you always saw fire engine red zonals combined with white allysum and trailing blue lobelia. It was patriotic, all right, but that look is now considered passé. Instead, gardeners are getting adventurous and combining zonals in knockout planting schemes.

❀ **Regals:** Also called Martha Washingtons. Similar to zonals, but with pointier leaves and less flamboyant flowers. Use them in the same way as zonals.

❀ **Cascading:** Spikier flowers. Develop quickly into big, bushy plants that trail prettily over the edges of pots. Good on their own in hanging baskets. Popular in Europe. Best bet for lazy gardeners, because garden centers often sell them ready-planted.

❀ **Ivy-leafed:** Pretty pointy leaves, like ivy, with spiky flowers. They can be cascading or have a more compact growth habit. Often more heat-tolerant than other varieties. Work well in both planters and smaller pots.

❀ **Scented:** Mostly ho-hum flowers, but the plants smell divine. Interesting foliage, often fuzzy-textured and fun to stroke. Good for semi-shady spots: the only geraniums that don't insist on full sun. Combine them with colorful annuals, in sniffing range and in spots where you can brush up against them to release the scent. Varieties to look for:

❀ *P. odoratissimum:* Known as the "apple geranium." A fave with Victorians. Fragrance of both apple and cinnamon.

❀ *P. capitatum* or Attar of Roses. Scent is just like roses. Needs a big pot.

> ## Hot tip
> "Even if you love white flowers, don't bother with white geraniums. When their petals drop, they go brown. These cling to the flower heads and look awful."
> —*Martin Knirr, geranium grower*

❀ *P. quercifolium* **'Chocolate-Mint':** Pretty, minty, with purple-streaked leaves. Some people swear they can also detect chocolate.

❀ *P. citrosa:* Strong citronella scent. Said to repel mosquitoes, but that's debatable.

❀ *P. 'Frensham':* Truly divine scent of lemons that's better than the real thing.

❀ *P. tomentosum:* The peppermint geranium. Velvety purplish green leaves. Good in hanging baskets. Nice minty smell.

Do

✓ Keep geraniums (except scented ones) in full sun. They won't flower well in shade.

✓ Water, but don't overdo it. Geraniums hate wet feet.

✓ Look for heat-tolerant varieties (check the labels).

✓ Nip off spent flower heads.

✓ Fertilize weekly with 20-20-20, starting in mid-summer.

Don't

✗ Don't pot up geraniums dry. Make sure the soil mass surrounding the roots is damp before transplanting into a bigger pot.

✗ Put geraniums outside in spring if the temperature is going to drop below 50°F/10°C.

✗ Expose young plants to cold winds.

✗ Feel you must rush them indoors before a light fall frost. Tough, mature plants can take a little bit of freezing (but not much).

Colorful combos

❀ Orange geraniums (preferably zonals) with a burgundy-colored coleus, a tall phormium in green and purple, and white impatiens or white browallia.

❀ A stellar geranium called Vancouver Centennial (which has orangey red flowers with exquisite brown and gold leaves) with trailing nasturtiums in red and chrome, the yellow-green foliage of *Helichrysum petiolare* Limelight, and spiky spider plants.

- Shocking pink geraniums with violet verbena, purple heliotrope, and dwarf white snapdragons (*Antirrhinum hispanicum*).
- A geranium variety called Freckles, which has rose-pink flowers daubed with white and deep pink, with silver-leaved licorice vine (*Helichrysum petiolare*) and purply blue pimpernel (*Anagallis monellii*) or blue fanflower (*Scaevola aemula*). Terrific in a gray pot.

Can I winter geraniums over outside?

Probably not. Geraniums are tropical flowers, originally from South Africa. They're generally hardy to about 35°F/2°C. Scented geraniums can sometimes be wintered over, in pots against a sunny wall, if you live where nighttime temperatures don't dip below 23°F/–5°C.

As for other varieties of geraniums, the best thing is to winter them over, still in their pots, in a cool, dry basement or garage. Prune the plants back to a few inches and don't water during this dormant period. However, since this procedure is out of the question in most condos and apartments, it's often best to simply buy new started geraniums every spring.

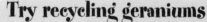

Try recycling geraniums

Here's a way to save money: every November, cut back your geraniums to 1 ft./30 cm high. Dig them out of window boxes and pack them tightly together into a plastic pot. Soak the pot thoroughly on the balcony. Then bring it in and store it on a dresser, away from the window. Water a bit, but not much.

In spring, cut back leggy new growth to 3 in./8 cm high and repot in fresh potting soil (three or four plants to each window box). Put them out on the balcony again.

Note: Gardening gurus consider this formula highly irregular. They take a different tack. Their suggestion:

Make stem cuttings 4 in./10 cm long several weeks before frost hits. Pot these up in new soil. Throw the mother plant out. Grow the babies on a sunny window ledge throughout the winter. Come spring, introduce them to the great green world.

The choice is yours.

How to Have Everything Coming Up Roses

Roses are romantic, but they tend to be finicky. While many balcony and rooftop gardeners dream of having lots of luscious roses tumbling over arbors and trellises, that dream can be hard to translate into reality. The unfortunate truth is, many roses aren't suitable for containers. They require full sun, heavy soil that drains well, and lots of room. Certain types of roses also don't take kindly to being left outside, with their roots above the ground, throughout the winter. However, you don't have to miss out on the undeniable elegance of these classic flowers. The trick is to pick the "toughies" that will adapt well to difficult conditions.

Resilient roses for balconies, rooftops, and courtyards

❁ **Hardy shrub roses**, especially those labeled "Parkland" or "Explorer." These types were developed in areas of Canada where winters are harsh (Winnipeg and Ottawa) and they're bred especially to cope with adverse conditions. For planting in containers, pick smaller varieties. Worth trying are Morden

Blush, which has lovely peachy blooms; Henry Hudson, with pinkish white flowers; and Champlain, which is dark red. To train up a trellis, try the shrub rose Alchymist.

- ❀ **Old-fashioned climbing roses** are great in a ground-floor courtyard. You can train them up trellises—they grow tall and will help make the place seem private. Worth trying are *Rosa* 'Alba', an ancient white rose; York and Lancaster, a fragrant damask that's white streaked with pink; and Evelyn, a David Austin climber. Their blooming period is, unfortunately, brief.

- ❀ **Ballerina,** a hybrid musk rose. Many balcony gardeners find this one takes to a container like a charm (but make sure the container is big). An import from England (first introduced in 1937), it forms a rounded shrub about 4 ft./125 cm in height, and its biggest plus is that it keeps on producing clusters of delightful pinkish white single blooms, edged with pink, for weeks on end. Ballerina is also somewhat fragrant.

> ### Hot tip
> "Roses like a good soak once a week, using the hose. Don't give them daily dribbles with the watering can."
> *Christopher Cantlon, condo rose grower*

- ❀ **Polyantha roses** perform particularly well on rooftops. They're low-growing and less affected by winds than taller roses. They bloom continuously all summer. The Fairy and Orange Triumph varieties are hardy and disease-resistant.

- ❀ ***Rosa rugosa,*** both the Alba (white) and Rubra (pink) varieties, are the toughest roses around. They grow wild along the eastern seaboard of North America and produce lovely bright orange hips the size of cherry tomatoes. Their delicious scent can be detected yards away. The drawback of *R. rugosa* is that the blooming period is often disappointingly short—and the rest of the year the bushes take up a lot of space and look quite homely. They also need big containers, as they spread rapidly.

- ❀ ***Rosa gallica*** is one of the few roses that will tolerate a bit of shade. It comes in several varieties; pick a compact one for a small space.

Making roses flourish

Do

✓ Buy roses from a reputable specialist rose nursery in your area and ask for advice on varieties that are suitable for containers or courtyards.

    ✓ Use big, roomy containers. The French Versailles type of planter (a big squarish box standing on legs) is ideal. So are old whiskey barrels. Fill them with a good, rich growing mix (see pages 33–35), and add several handfuls of bone meal to the mix. Be prepared to replace the soil every few years.

    ✓ Plant in early fall. That way, roses have a chance to settle into their new surroundings before winter freeze-up—and as a result, they will often adapt better to summer's heat the following year.

    ✓ When planting roses in cold climates, always position the crown (the lumpy bit, where the stem meets the roots) 1 to 2 in./2.5 to 5 cm *below* the surface of the soil. This applies equally whether you're planting in the ground or in containers. (Misleading advice is sometimes given on plant tags and in garden center catalogs.)

✓ Mound up the soil around the stem right after planting. (This applies whether you're planting in a container or the ground.) Leave the soil mounded up all winter.

✓ Water thoroughly after planting. Not once, but twice. One condo gardener (who is an expert at growing roses) recommends positioning the rosebush in its hole, filling with soil halfway up the sides, then watering. Once the hole is filled to the top, water again.

✓ Come summer, prune off dead flowers right after they've finished blooming. Don't leave them on the stems.

Don't

✗ Buy hybrid tea roses. They're sold everywhere and often make a promising start, but they develop problems later on. These roses are notoriously prone to diseases such as mildew and black spot and usually require constant fussing.

✗ Leave container-grown roses outside all winter, unprotected, and expect them to survive (see page 134).

Plant miniature roses

Also called "patio roses," minis are inexpensive and surprisingly tough. Many garden centers sell them ready-planted in pots. Their small, dainty double blooms come in shades like pink, cherry red, and salmon and they look charming mixed with annual flowers of a similar size. Minis will grow like gangbusters in an environment that suits them and often winter over happily on a balcony. But they are so reasonably priced, some gardeners find it simpler to just buy new ones every spring.

Summer Bulbs: Exotic and Different

For years, the only bulbs grown by most gardeners were the kind you plant in the fall: tulips, daffodils, crocuses, and so on. But now summer-blooming tropical bulbs are all the rage, and that's good news for people gardening in condos, apartment buildings, and other small spaces. These types of bulbs are perfectly suited to cultivating in containers. Most start producing gorgeous flowers quickly and will continue to put on a show all summer.

Buy summer bulbs in spring. They're sold at most garden centers. Some look bulb-like; others are elongated tubers or hard little rhizomes in green or brown. Most come packed in sawdust shavings in net bags. Press the bulby and tuberous ones with a finger; they should be firm and full, with no squashy or dried-out bits. (You can also buy from specialist nurseries by mail order. They tend to be more expensive, but the selection and quality is better.) Plant early in spring in a light, soil-less mix (follow instructions as to depth and spacing), and keep them indoors on a sunny window ledge for a few weeks. Don't put them outside until all frosts have finished. If you have no indoor facilities, it's a good idea to look for pre-started plants; otherwise, you'll wait till mid or late summer for flowers. Fertilize every two weeks. In the right kind of conditions—they like heat, with plenty of moisture—many summer bulbs grow with gusto.

Bulbous beauties to try

❀ **Achimenes** (pronounced *ack-im-en-EES*): Produces pretty, jewel-like 2 in./5 cm blooms in red, pink, or apricot for weeks on end. Slow to get started. Will tolerate a bit of shade.

❀ **Begonias:** Dismissed as "old ladies' plants" for years, begonias are back in a big way. Most garden centers sell pre-started tuberous kinds in pink, yellow, orange, or red. Buy these if you want quick results (replant in bigger pots). They will bloom non-stop all summer. For hanging baskets, look for small trailing begonias and picotee varieties (which means petals with a contrasting color

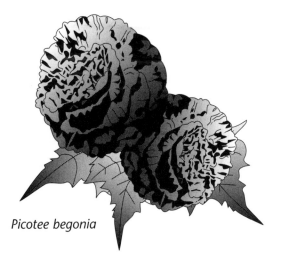

Picotee begonia

around the edge—very fetching). But what's even hotter are non-tuberous begonias, which often have interesting flowers *and* fantastic foliage. Look for Dragon's Wing, Angel Wing, and Holly Leaf kinds. The biggest plus of all begonias is that they thrive in shade.

❀ **Calla lilies (*Zantedeschia*):** Fashionable, but often finicky. Large, shiny blooms shaped like trumpets and exotic dark green foliage, often spotted with white. Good on balconies because they can cope with windy locations. They don't produce as many flower heads as other summer-flowering bulbs, but are spectacular when they do unfurl themselves. Don't confuse callas with cannas.

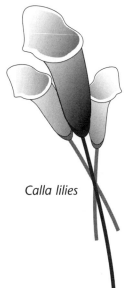

Calla lilies

- ❀ **Canna lilies:** Oh-so-trendy right now, these knockout plants grow huge, with whacking great leaves and brilliant flowers, usually in reds or oranges. Pick the ones with striped foliage, not plain green, and give them lots of room. Cannas can be frustrating, because they take a while to develop. (Start them indoors, if you can.) They can reach 6 ft./2 m high and need sun.

- ❀ **Dahlias:** Consigned to the compost heap for decades, but now gardeners are drooling over dahlias again. In containers, skip the huge, showy blooms (which need propping up with ugly sticks) and go for smaller varieties like Bonne Esperance, which has pink daisy-like flowers, or Kasagi, deep orange and red. Dahlias with burgundy foliage, such as Japanese Bishop, are in vogue (combine them with the leaves of canna lilies). They all like sun and won't bloom till late summer.

- ❀ **Ismene (*Hymenocallis*):** Don't confuse this one with *Hemerocallis*, which are daylilies. You see *Hymenocallis* a lot on Caribbean islands. They have flaring, fragrant blooms in white or yellow that look a bit like daffodils and make a fantastic display in mid-summer. They prefer light, filtered shade.

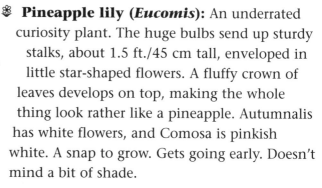

- ❀ **Pineapple lily (*Eucomis*):** An underrated curiosity plant. The huge bulbs send up sturdy stalks, about 1.5 ft./45 cm tall, enveloped in little star-shaped flowers. A fluffy crown of leaves develops on top, making the whole thing look rather like a pineapple. Autumnalis has white flowers, and Comosa is pinkish white. A snap to grow. Gets going early. Doesn't mind a bit of shade.

When winter comes

Bring summer bulbs indoors and store them— still in their containers—in a cool, dry place. Centrally heated condos and apartments get too hot. An unheated garage or locker is good (but never

Eucomis

expose bulbs to freezing temperatures). Let the containers dry out, then next spring add a bit of fresh potting soil, water thoroughly, and put out on the balcony again.

If you don't have a cool storage space, forget trying to winter over summer bulbs on a window ledge or in a cupboard. They probably won't do well. Unfortunately, it's best to throw them out and simply buy new bulbs next year.

Hot tip

"Look for big begonia and dahlia tubers. They'll produce more flowers."

—Dugald Cameron, bulb expert

Herbs Make Great Scents for Beginners

Ask experienced balcony gardeners what they grew first and most of them say the same thing: herbs. They're perfect container plants. Mostly hassle-free, they look and smell good—and they don't take up too much space. It's also fun to have fresh herbs close at hand to use in cooking.

If you have a hankering for herbs, however, remember that nearly all of them like sun. Lots of it. Many originate in Mediterranean countries like Greece and Italy, and they don't take kindly to shady locations. If your balcony, courtyard, or rooftop doesn't get sunshine five or six hours a day, forget herbs. They'll look lousy and leggy (and are also prone to attacks by bugs or fungal diseases).

Here are a few tips for success with herbs:

Do
✓ Buy a growing mix that contains perlite or vermiculite, because herbs need good drainage.
✓ Add a scoop of coarse, gritty sand (get it at a builder's yard) to your growing mix, if you can. Most herbs like sandy soil.
✓ Buy herbs as started plants. All of them (except dill) take too long to raise from seed.
✓ Water regularly and position herbs in the sunniest spot.
✓ Grow herbs together in the same pot. Combine different textures and colors. Gray-leaved sage, for instance, looks great with parsley and lemon thyme.
✓ Mix herbs with other plants. The trailing ones, like thyme, make a great mulch around the base of pots.

✓ Experiment. Herb growers keep coming out with amazing variations on tried and true stalwarts.

✓ Position herbs where you can bury your nose in them and brush legs and arms up against them.

✓ Crush herbs between your thumb and forefinger. It's the best way to release the scent.

✓ Snip young leaves off for salads and cooked dishes. Old ones get tough.

Don't

✗ Let herbs flower if you want to use them in the kitchen. Keep pinching the flower heads off.

✗ Grow mint and oregano in the same container as other plants. Both are bossy, with roots that spread everywhere. (Plant mint in a ground-floor courtyard and you will never get rid of it.)

Eight easy herbs

❀ **Basil:** This fave comes in more than thirty-five varieties now. There's Thai basil, Greek basil, African blue basil, Genovese basil—the list goes on. Confused? Then opt for plain old sweet basil (*Ocimum basilicum*), which is still one of the best. If you intend to dry it, get the smaller-leaved variety *O. basilicum minimum*. Basil is an annual: it will turn black when frost hits.

❀ **Chives:** Pretty plant, great for cooks. Pick a few long strands at a time and snip them into dishes. Include the violet flowers: they taste surprisingly good. Try flat-leaved garlic chives (*Allium tuberosum*), which have a stronger flavor and aren't as invasive as regular chives. In fall, prune chives back hard, dig up a section of the roots, replant them in a new pot, and bring indoors. You'll soon have fresh new leaves to snip off throughout the winter.

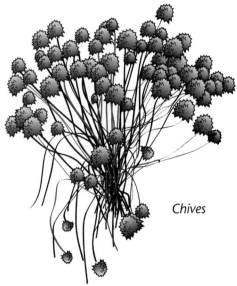

Chives

❅ **Dill (*Anethum graveolens*):** Annual, grows tall, and can look untidy on a balcony. It also self-seeds everywhere. To avoid a dilly deluge, pick leaves early, before the big flower heads develop (they taste best when they're small, anyway).

❅ **Italian parsley (*Petroselinum crispum neapolitanum*):** This flat-leaved variety is said to have better flavor than the common curly-leaved kind (though that's debatable). Parsley is a biennial, but it's best to buy new plants every spring, as older plants get tough and taste bitter.

❅ **Oregano:** A perennial and a must in Italian cooking, but there's a lot of awful oregano around. Make sure you buy the variety *Origanum* Kaliteri, which the Greeks grow. Can be wintered over indoors, but tends to get straggly. Try leaving it outside, with a protective mulch.

❅ **Rosemary:** Beautiful fragrant herb, with gray-green spiky leaves and violet flowers. Shear it back in the autumn and winter it over indoors, preferably in a cool, dry place. (It often gets mildew inside homes that are too warm or where there is insufficient light.)

❅ **Sage (*Salvia officinalis*):** Good-looking container plant that can grow 2 ft./60 cm high. Try variegated sages too, which have pretty lime green edges. (Russian sage, *Perovskia atriplicifolia,* a recent hot herb, is ornamental too, but not really a sage.) A perennial, sage can winter out of doors in many locations. Don't prune it too fiercely in spring. Leave the old woody bits on the plant. Just cut off the dead stems.

❅ **English thyme (*Thymus vulgaris*):** The compact form is best for containers. But if you have space, try lemon

Start small

Grow only a few favorite herbs that you know you'll use. It's easy to get carried away at the garden center and buy ten different kinds of basil. Then you get home and wonder what to do with them.

thyme and orange spice thyme (with gorgeous scents; use them fresh, not dried, in soups and fish and chicken dishes) and woolly thyme (*T. pseudolaginosus*).

Unusual herbs to try

- **Beefsteak plant (*Perilla frutescens*):** Misnamed (it has nothing to do with tomatoes), this tall purple-leaved annual is the "shiso" of Japanese cuisine (served fresh or pickled to accompany sushi or sashimi). It makes a lovely backdrop to many flowers, and is very easy to grow.

- **Bergamot (*Monarda didyma*):** The secret "scent" in Earl Grey tea. Pretty red or pink tufty flowers, which attract bees and look lovely in containers. Delicious fragrance. Perennial. Grow where there's good air circulation. It often gets mildew and is best planted behind a shorter flower (so its affected stems are hidden). Winter outside, covered in mulch.

- **Hyssop (*Agastache*):** A pretty herb, with fronds of flowers in purple (also other colors). Easy to grow, but dislikes it wet. Attracts butterflies. Grow as an annual in northern climates.

- **Sweet herb of Paraguay, or sugar leaf (*Stevia rebaudiana*):** Nothing special to look at, but a novelty. It contains steviaside, which is a hundred times sweeter than sugar. Soon, stevia may replace those little pink packets of Sweet'N Low found on fast-food counters. In the meantime, dry the leaves and crumble them into coffee or add them to pies. They taste faintly of cinnamon and certainly are sweet. Bring indoors for the winter.

- **Vietnamese coriander (*Polygonum odoratum*):** Not a pretty herb, but a great alternative to regular coriander (*Eryngium foetidum*), which is tedious to grow. (You have to keep planting new seed all summer.) The Vietnamese version gives the same zip to Mexican and Indian dishes as those bunches of regular coriander sold in supermarkets. It's a tropical plant, related to a common weed found in North America. Grows easily, with a trailing habit. Plant in a wide container. Cut back and bring indoors in the fall.

Yes, You Can Grow Veggies

There's an undeniable thrill in eating something that you've grown yourself. A plain tomato, picked fresh off the vine and sliced while it's still warm from the sun, tastes better than the most exotic, expensive vegetable or fruit sold at the supermarket. Crisp, just-pulled greens, rinsed clean and added to a salad or a stir fry, are also hard to beat.

Many people with small gardens miss out on this experience because they presume that their balcony, terrace, or courtyard isn't big enough for vegetables. They're probably mistaken. You can usually squeeze in something—even if it's just one tomato plant or a bit of Swiss chard. And who wants to be drowning in zucchini as big as baseball bats anyway? Traditional vegetable gardens, with everything planted in rows, may yield a lot to eat, but they're a huge amount of work, and their owners usually wind up giving most of the stuff away at the end of the summer. By contrast, a few veggies cultivated in containers are fun. The taste treats may be few and far between, but that makes them all the more delectable. And don't worry about the aesthetic aspect of vegetables. Contrary to popular opinion, most aren't plug ugly. Some veggies can look surprisingly decorative, intermingled with flowers.

Does the sun shine in?

If it doesn't, forget virtually all vegetables. Their one essential requirement is full, unobstructed sunlight for at least six hours a day. A balcony or courtyard that faces south-east with no concrete overhang is the best location, because vegetables want to bask in the glow of that big, round orb the moment it appears over the horizon. A southern aspect is fine too (though, in some areas, it can get too hot and dry). If you face west, and the sun doesn't swing around to your condo or apartment until noon, some veggies are probably still a possibility—so long as you have uninterrupted sunshine until the evening.

Then there's the wind...
Constant breezes can actually be a plus, because most vegetables benefit from good air circulation. However, very high winds will damage and burn plant stems and leaves—and may prevent some veggies from growing at all. If you have a windy balcony or rooftop, consider putting up screens to protect your plants (see pages 22–23).

...And the water
Most vegetables get thirsty quickly. Without sufficient moisture, leafy ones (like lettuce) will taste bitter when they mature, and those that produce tubers (like beets) won't develop properly. You need to water often—and deeply. It also helps to put mulch around the base of plants to conserve moisture.

...And the soil
You can't get away with so-so soil, because veggies are greedy: most gobble up more nutrients than flowers. Buy a bagged growing medium that's formulated for vegetables (it will have fertilizers added). If you can't find one, get a mix that contains peat moss, vermiculite, and perlite, with some composted manure. Then be prepared to juice up this concoction with fertilizers regularly. Look for a fertilizer that's designed for the vegetables you are growing. Use it every week. (Tomatoes require a different formula from leafy vegetables because they set fruit.)

You also need big, deep containers for most vegetables. Planters at least 2 ft./60 cm long are terrific (you can mix some herbs in too). So are whiskey barrels.

Eight veggies to try

❀ **Beans:** The bush variety (which we buy in stores) won't work in containers. But Scarlet Runner beans do—and their red flowers provide lovely dabs of color. Give them a trellis or strings to climb up and they're as eye-catching as any clematis. Soak the bean seeds in tepid water for twenty-four hours before planting and you'll get quicker results. Be sure to pick Scarlet Runner bean pods early. They get stringy and tough if they're are left on the vine too long. Blue Lake, another climbing bean, is less fibrous, but not as pretty. It has white flowers.

❀ **Beets:** Will grow in a deep container. One of the few veggies that tolerates a bit of shade. Scatter the seeds on the top of your pots. Add just a smidgen of soil to cover them. Lots of seedlings will come up. Keep thinning these to just two or three plants; otherwise, the beet bit under the soil won't get a chance to expand. (The easiest way to do this is with a pair of nail scissors. Yanking out unwanted seedlings with your fingers will disturb the seedlings you want to leave behind.) The crimson-edged leaves and magenta stems are colorful in a container. You can also pick the young leaves and eat them (in salads or steamed) while the rest is developing.

❀ **Garlic:** A conversation piece on a balcony, because garlic stems can grow 8 ft/2.5 m high, and they develop incredibly curly flower stalks. (Plant them behind something else.) People think garlic is too fiddly, but it's easy—and fun. Simply plant single cloves, with the skin still attached, 4 to 6 in./10 to 15 cm below the soil in a deep planter, *during the fall*. They need good, rich soil. (Buy a garlic variety that's grown in your area, not the supermarket kind.) If you have long freezing winters, wrap the container (see pages 134–35). Wait till spring. The corn-like way that garlic shoots up is astonishing. Harvest the mature bulb late that summer, when the stems are turning brown. But in a windy location, forget garlic—its tall stalks may snap.

❀ **Lettuce:** Does well for some people, poorly for others. In containers, it prefers a bit of shade (a too sunny location will make it bolt). A variety called Grand Rapids keeps producing leaves instead of maturing into a heart, so you can keep picking it. Use started plants rather than seed.

❀ **Onions:** Can be picky about soil and moisture—and slow to mature. Green onions are easiest. Buy started seedlings, trim them back by one-third, and plant early in the spring, with the top bit of the bulb sticking up above the soil surface.

❀ **Swiss chard:** A truly super veggie. Much better for balconies than spinach because it will carry on growing all summer, whatever the weather. It's also highly decorative. Try a variety called Bright Lights, which boasts stems in an amazing array of colors: white, red, yellow, pink, or orange. Plant chard early in spring (but it won't sulk if you don't get around to it until early summer) and thin to a couple of plants. They're ample for several people. Just cut leaves off as you need them and steam or stir fry with onion and butter. Eat the stems too. They're surprisingly tender and actually taste as good as the leaves. A trailing herb (like thyme) looks pretty growing around the base of a chard plant.

❀ **Tomatoes:** For container growing, the cherry kind work best. (Big beefsteaky types of tomatoes need lots of space and don't usually produce many fruits in containers.) A variety called Tiny Tim is sold everywhere, but look for Sweet 100, a prolific provider of yummy little fruits. Buy started tomato plants rather than seeds (which take too long to develop for most condo and apartment dwellers). Put only one tomato plant in a pot at least 1 ft./30 cm in diameter and provide a stake or a wire cage for support. Plastic protective sleeves (which you fill with water) are a good idea in areas with late spring frosts.

You can also train tomatoes up a trellis. Tie the central tomato stem to the trellis with something soft like panty-hose or strips of rag. Then keep nipping out the side shoots to stop the plant getting bushy.

Leave tomatoes on the vine as long as you can. When frost is threatening, harvest right away or cover with a blanket at night. While tomatoes appreciate fertilizer, be careful of any product that's high in nitrogen. (It's the first number in fertilizer formulas, for instance, 20-10-10.) You'll wind up with a big leafy plant—and few fruits. And leave *Lycopersicon esculentum* (the lovely Latin mouthful of a name for tomatoes) off your gardening list if you have any shade at all. This is one veggie that demands a front and center situation in the sun.

❀ **Zucchini:** If you have lots of space on a rooftop, try one. (But only one. They grow huge.) In a whiskey barrel or big planter, zucchini leaves can look as decorative as any expensive shrub—and they make an impact quickly. Plant three seeds. Thin to a single plant when it's about 4 in./ 10 cm tall. Look for compact varieties with interesting "fruit." Jaguar produces shiny dark green zucchinis. Those of Golden Dawn are a yummy yellow (and they're fun to watch, spiking out from the plant). Pollination may be a problem on very tall high-rises. If you get leaves but nothing else, you may be too high in the sky for pollinating insects to fly in and work their magic.

Three to avoid

❀ **Corn:** Grows too tall. Tends to blow over. Try only if you have a sheltered position and tons of space.
❀ **Spinach:** Bolts when weather turns hot. Swiss chard tastes better anyway.
❀ **Squash:** Fall varieties, that is. (Zucchini is a type of squash.) They ramble everywhere and need a long growing season. (But if you have a rooftop where it can spread, try a variety called Cream of the Crop in a *very* big container.)

When summer's over

Remove the leftover veggie stalks, haul them off to a friend's compost heap, and put ornamental kale and cabbages on the menu instead. Both are delish as new decorative plants in your containers.

Pre-started ornamental kale plants come in yummy colors—pale greens, violets, pinks, purples—with fantastic, frilly shapes. Cabbages are usually smaller, with smooth, rounded leaves, and their centers often resemble delicate pink or cream roses.

Buy plump specimens with lots of healthy-looking leaves. Position them at an angle in the containers so you can see their showy flower heads from the front. (Some growers are now producing ornamental cabbage and kale with curving stems so gardeners don't have to do this.) Add a few pansies. Enjoy the display for weeks. All these plants can take a bit of frost and may last a long time, depending on the climate. (But don't be tempted to eat the kale and cabbages. They taste like shoe leather.)

Try rhubarb

Rhubarb is getting pricey (and hard to find) in supermarket produce sections. If you love this spring fruit and have lots of sun, try growing your own in a big container. The leaves are very decorative—and you can make a pie from the stalks to impress your friends.

Rhubarb

Grow Up: Make Maximum Use of Your Space

Think about growing up—that is, choosing vines that climb vertically. This kind of greenery is especially useful in a tiny space, but it can look wonderful in any outdoor area, large or small. North American gardeners tend to overlook vines, yet in Britain, they clamber everywhere—over gates and archways, up walls, fences, and drainage pipes. They look terrific too. The Brits, a nation of savvy gardeners crowded together on an island, undoubtedly learned long ago that if you have no room to spread outwards, you can always go upwards.

Aside from the aesthetic aspect, there are many pluses to vines. Plants that creep, weave, twine, or cling are often easy to grow; they send forth plenty of greenery (and hence add oxygen to the air); they muffle sound from the street; they provide a sense of enclosure. But their most appealing feature in our crowded cities is that they make great privacy screens. Your little oasis will seem less open and unprotected (and neighbors less intrusive) if you include a couple of vines. It's definitely worth the effort to grow them.

Vines do take a bit of effort. While a few will cling unassisted to walls and balcony railings (or trail nicely out of window boxes), most need some kind of support. And on balconies or rooftops high off the ground, watch out for the wind. It can be so fierce it will rip vines with slender, fragile stems (like clematis) right off trellises.

Honeysuckle

How to grow vines

Do

✓ First check that they are permitted. Some buildings forbid residents to grow certain types of vines on the grounds that the clinging foliage may wreck masonry or ramble everywhere and upset neighbors. (These fears are often unfounded, but it can be hard to convince people otherwise.)

✓ Inform your neighbors. Don't just go ahead and plant.

✓ Before buying, consider if you have space to attach a trellis. On open balconies, particularly those backed by big plate glass windows, there's often nowhere to hang up anything, not even one hook—in which case, you'll probably have to settle for vines grown on free-standing supports (or skip them entirely).

✓ Make all supports portable, in case you move. Simple trellises, fashioned from crisscrossed slats of wood, are sold at home renovation stores everywhere. Look for one called Double Six. It's recommended by many balcony gardeners. Hang the prefabricated sections, which usually measure 6 ft./ 2 m by 4 ft./125 cm, from walls on big hooks. Make sure hooks are firmly screwed into the wall. Use wall plugs in concrete and masonry. Also in vogue: trellises made from metals like copper and iron, fashioned into squiggly shapes.

✓ Make inexpensive free-standing supports from bare tree branches, gathered in spring. (They should have plenty of twiggy bits.) Press branches firmly into pots and train vines up them. Some people pull the branches together at the top, and tie them together. This makes a pleasing obelisk shape. You can also buy wrought-iron obelisks, which look elegant but are expensive.

✓ Prune vines back if they get too unruly.

✓ Check out tropical vines, which must be brought indoors during the winter in northern climates. Some inspired choices: winter jasmine (*Jasminum polyanthum*); mandevilla (sometimes known by an older name, *Dipladenia*); and passion flower (*Passiflora*), which can be annual or perennial.

Don't

✗ Bother with wisteria. It's beautiful, but frustrating. Many of these vines never flower, even after years of TLC.

✗ Scrimp. All vines do best in big, roomy containers filled with good growing mix. For flowering vines like clematis, add generous handfuls of bone meal to the mix (but don't do it if you live in an area where squirrels are a nuisance. See page 130).

✗ Wait till a vine is rambling everywhere before putting up something to support it. Hang up trellises in advance. You'll damage the plant doing it afterwards.

✗ Grow invasive vines. Many factors play a role in determining how big a plant will grow, but in areas with long, hot summers, you may be wise to avoid

> ❀ Boston ivy (*Parthenocissus tricuspidata*)
> ❀ Common hops (*Humulus lupulus*)
> ❀ Kudzu (*Pueraria lobata*)
> ❀ Dutchman's pipe (*Aristolochia durior*)
> ❀ Silver lace vine (*Polygonum aubertii*)
> ❀ Trumpet vine (*Campsis radicans*)
> ❀ Virginia creeper (*Parthenocissus quinquefolia*)

String your beans

Buy some jute string in a natural color. Lengths of it, stretched from hooks, provide a cheap support for many light annual vines, such as Scarlet Runner beans. Avoid plastic string in lurid colors. Take down the string in fall.

Pretty perennial climbers

Most perennial vines need something substantial to climb on. If the support isn't solid enough, they are liable to collapse after a few years' growth. Remember too that you'll have leave these vines outside in their containers all winter, and that most need some protection (see pages 134–35).

❀ **Bittersweet vine (*Celastrus scandens*):** In gardens this can ramble everywhere, but it's well mannered in a container. The spring flowers are nothing special, but come fall, golden foliage and clusters of scarlet berries are to die for. Be sure to buy a female plant (look for 'Diane' on the label) or you won't get that spectacular fruit. ('Hercules' is the male version. He does not produce berries.)

❀ **Clematis:** An oh-so-fashionable vine that comes in more varieties than Heinz. A good bet for balcony gardeners because it doesn't mind a bit of shade and usually isn't a rampant grower. (But there are exceptions. If you want a quick privacy screen, try clematis varieties called *tangutica* or late-summer-flowering *fargesioides*. They grow quicker than others, often into huge tangles of greenery. Whack them back if they get out of hand.) Experts invariably claim that clematis is easy to grow, but it often isn't. Most varieties do best in a protected location with early morning sun. If you're high on an exposed balcony that faces west, you may find that the fragile stems get ripped off trellises by the wind. Always shield the roots of clematis with another plant, give them some kind of support, and keep them moist. Entire books are written about clematis varieties and their peculiar pruning requirements. If you're a beginner, stick to a classic variety, *C. jackmanii*, which produces pretty purple blooms in mid-summer. Cut the stick-like stems back to 1 ft./30 cm high every spring.

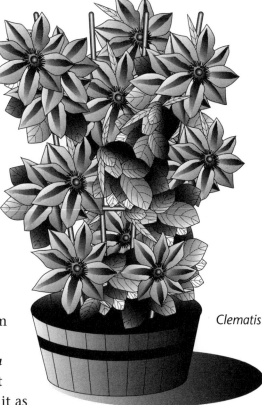

Clematis

❀ **Climbing hydrangea (*Hydrangea anomala petiolaris*):** This is a great vine if you have shade, but don't use it as a privacy screen: it takes too long to get going. Some keep their owners in suspense for years before producing their first flowers. Has dark leaves with pretty, lacy white flowers, which are more prolific in sun. On a brick or concrete wall, it will cling without any means of support. (A relative, Japanese hydrangea vine (*Schizophragma hydrangeoides*) gets going quicker, but is hard to find at garden centres).

❀ **English ivy (*Hedera helix*):** A classic climbing plant with shiny green leaves. Beloved by the Brits, who cover walls with it. Be warned, however: ivy can be hard to grow in areas of North America that get long, cold winters. It often dies off (even though plant catalogs claim it's "hardy").

❀ **Euonymus:** There are climbing varieties (see pages 99–100).

❀ **Five-leaved Akebia:** Originally from Asia, it's often called "the chocolate vine" because of its brown stems. Has fragrant purplish flowers in spring, but grow this one for its pretty, semi-evergreen leaves, which have five segments. Akebia can be too pushy, but shouldn't be a problem in containers—and it makes a good privacy screen.

❀ **Honeysuckle (*Lonicera*):** The glorious scent of honeysuckle flowers in mornings and evenings is one of gardening's delights. Hummingbirds love it. Be sure to pick a variety called Gold Flame if you want fragrance. Another popular variety, Dropmore Scarlet, is prettier, with scarlet flowers, but has no scent. Position in full sun and don't grow honeysuckle unless you have lots of space.

❀ **Porcelain berry (*Ampelopsis brevipedunculata*):** No one had heard of this vine a decade ago. Now you see it everywhere, with good reason. It has unusual foliage in green, white, and pink and its berries, produced in fall, are an extraordinary electric blue-purple. It can be difficult to grow.

Easy annual vines

The best way to grow most of these is from seed. Started plants will produce flowers quicker, but the seedlings of annual vines often don't take kindly to being transplanted. They all prefer full sun.

- 🌸 **Black-eyed Susan vine (*Thunbergia alata*):** Has delightful orange flowers with black centers. Needs support on a wall, but can also be used in hanging baskets.

- 🌸 **Cup and saucer vine (*Cobaea scandens*):** Deserves to be better known. A Mexican native, with pretty purple flowers. Climbs by tendrils that push out everywhere. Give it a trellis for support. (Don't try to start this one from seed unless you have a nighttime temperature of at least 70°F/20°C.)

> ## Hot tip
>
> "In cold climates, plant vines several inches deeper than gardening books say, and mound earth up around them before winter. This works particularly well for clematis."
>
> —Elsa Young, condo clematis grower

- 🌸 **Morning glories (*Ipomoea*):** Garden mainstays, perfect for containers. They twine themselves nicely up strings. Flower colors range from white to pale pink to a lurid turquoise. A relative, moonflower vine, produces white flowers that open at night—and have a glorious scent. Plant it in sniffing range. It's okay to buy moonflower vine pre-started. You'll get flowers quicker.

- 🌸 **Red bean (*Dolichos lablab*):** A fast-growing annual vine that produces gorgeous pinkish purple flowers. Needs some kind of support. You can also eat the beans.

- 🌸 **Scarlet runner beans (*Phaseolus coccineus*):** See pages 85–86.

Morning glory

Shrubs: Great Shapes, Great Styles

Many people overlook shrubs because they presume "bushes" are boring. They aren't. Planted in containers, the blocky shapes of shrubs will add symmetry and style to your balcony. Shrubs also function well as backdrops to displays of perennials and annuals—and some of them, particularly flowering ones, are outstanding showpieces grown on their own.

The other wonderful advantage of shrubs is that most are low maintenance. In the fiddling and fussing department, shrubs win hands down over most flowers, perennial or annual. In many cases, you simply plant shrubs, water deeply—and that's it.

However, these kinds of plants do have drawbacks, particularly for balcony gardeners. Most shrubs have a bushy growth habit. They shoot out stems that (usually) turn into woody branches as they age, and these branches keep on multiplying. So, over time, shrubs will outgrow containers. They also require pruning to keep their shape. If you're looking for a suitable shrub, always seek out those two magic words, "compact" and "dwarf." And remember that if shrubs do get too big, you may have to divide them.

Many popular shrubs also can't take long cold winters in containers, especially in exposed locations. Be sure to ask at the garden center if the shrub you are thinking of buying will be hardy in a container in your area. If they tell you it's "borderline hardy," be sure to wrap the shrub up in some protective insulation for the winter (see page 135).

Some shrubs to try

🍀 **Anthony Waterer spirea (*Spiraea* x *bumalda* 'Anthony Waterer'):** One of the easiest shrubs in the world to grow. Bursts forth with bubble gum pink flowers and lime green leaves in early spring. Use a big container; it spreads rapidly and can grow to about 3 ft./1 m or taller. Tolerates some shade, but needs sun to flower prolifically. When it's getting too big for the container, simply tip it out and hack it in half. It is as tough as old boots and tolerates all kinds of abuse. Look also for a relative, Gold Flame spirea. It's easy to grow, too.

2006

🍀 **Deutzia:** A durable, attractive shrub that doesn't get enough recognition from gardeners. Try a compact variety, *Deutzia* x *lemoinei* 'Compacta', which produces scads of pretty white flowers in spring and grows to about 4 ft./125 cm high, or the smaller Nikko Slender deutzia (*Deutzia gracilis* 'Nikko').

🍀 **Hydrangeas:** Can be difficult in containers, because they like it damp and are fussy about soil. The fashionable lace-cap varieties, *Hydrangea macrophylla*, seem particularly picky. Try instead Pee Wee oakleaf hydrangea, *Hydrangea quercifolia*, which blooms late in the summer, or another Pee Wee, *Hydrangea paniculata* 'Pink Diamond'. In locations they like, these shrubs can grow huge, with long-lasting decorative flowers (which look good in winter too).

🍀 **Miss Kim dwarf lilac (*Syringa patula* 'Miss Kim'):** Most lilacs grow too tall and wide for balconies. This one will reach about 6.5 ft./2 m, and it tolerates cold well. It has fragrant bluish flowers. Prune off dead flower heads immediately after flowering, or blooms will be sparse next year.

🍀 **Purple leaf sand cherry (*Prunus cistena*):** Reddish purple foliage with white flowers in spring. A good background shrub to other plants. Tough and easy to grow.

🍀 **Royal Purple smoke tree (*Cotinus coggyria*):** Deep purple foliage from May to September, with yellow-gray flower heads that resemble puffs of smoke. It looks sensational combined with *Weigela florida* 'Variegata'.

❀ **Seven-son flower** *(Heptacodium miconioides)*: A hot new import from China, this is well worth trying in a big container. It has some big pluses: creamy white fragrant flowers that bloom in late summer (when other bushy shrubs are looking blah), spectacular fall color, and attractive bark (which peels off). It's also hardy in northern climates. Needs watering often.

❀ **Shrubby cinquefoil** *(Potentilla fruticosa)*: Some gardeners turn their noses up at this garden stalwart because of its itty-bitty leaves and unremarkable chrome or pale yellow flowers. However, if you don't have much space, potentillas are perfect: unlike many other shrubs (and perennials), they keep on blooming merrily all summer. Another advantage is that potentillas are tough and hardy in most regions. They grow slowly, up to 4 ft./125 cm high, and need full sun to flower well. For a variation on the usual yellows, try Abbotsford, with pretty white flowers and bluish green leaves; Red Ace for reddish yellow flowers and a low growth habit; and Pink Beauty for clear pink flowers.

❀ **Weigela:** Many gardeners despise weigela (pronounced wee-GHEEL-a) because the beet red flowers of a variety called Bristol Ruby look lurid. Try instead *W. florida* 'Variegata', which has lovely pale pink flowers and green leaves edged with white; *W. florida* 'Wine and Roses', whose leaves are a spectacular burgundy purple, offsetting the rosy pink flowers; or a new dwarf variety, *W. florida* 'Midnight Wine', which looks similar to Wine and Roses.

Shrubs that stay green year round

The shrubs listed above are deciduous, which means they lose their leaves (and admittedly look pretty boring) in winter. That's why many gardeners like to include some evergreen shrubs. There are two different kinds of evergreens: conifers (which include spruces, pines, cedars, and junipers; most have spiky gray-green needles) and broadleaf evergreens (which are shrubs with regular-looking leaves that stay on the plant year-round). Many evergreens do well in containers. When buying any kind of evergreen, be sure to check if it is hardy in your area. Some are surprisingly sensitive to frost damage and may require winter protection (see page 135–36).

Conifers
* **Cedars** (*Thuja occidentalis*): A variety called Little Giant Globe grows to about 2.5 ft./75 cm high and a perfect globe shape. There are also taller kinds, if you have space.
* **Junipers:** Popular with landscapers, these are used around public buildings everywhere because they with-stand rough treatment, spread nicely, and look good in winter. There are many choices, but on a balcony, go for small, slow-growing varieties like Blue Star (*Juniperus squamata*), which has dense steel-blue foliage; 'Compact Andorra (*Juniperus horizontalis* 'Plumosa Compacta'), which is gray-green; and Dwarf Japanese Garden (*Juniperus procumbens* 'Nana'), with unusual tufty foliage that's blue-green. Sniff junipers closely before buying them. Some have an unpleasant smell, like cat spray.
* **Spruces:** Spruces are primarily trees, but some have a shrubby growth habit. One good choice is Little Gem (*Picea abies*), which develops into a nice, globe-shaped mound. Tree-sized conifers are covered on pages 105–7.

Broadleaf evergreens
* **Daphne (*Daphne cneorum*):** A pretty, low shrub with rose pink flowers that are fragrant. Very hardy, but keep it moist. It doesn't like to dry out. A relative, *Daphne burk-woodii* 'Carol Mackie', is even prettier, but not as hardy.
* **Euonymus (*Euonymus fortunei*):** These spreading shrubs are also loved for their toughness by professional landscapers. (If you live in a high-rise with landscaping around it, take a hard look. There's probably euonymus growing somewhere.) They also look colorful year round and don't mind shade. On a balcony, plant euonymus at the front of a big container and put something taller behind it. Compact varieties are good as edging plants

in ground-floor courtyards. If you like things neat, don't be afraid to prune euonymus. Cut off the straggly "spikes" that shoot out from the center and give the rest of the shrub an occasional haircut. Caution: Euonymus is sometimes attacked by scale (see page 126).

These euonymus varieties are all good in containers:

- ❀ Emerald Gaiety: Very popular, with green and white leaves. Goes with anything.
- ❀ Emerald 'n' Gold: Similar to Emerald Gaiety but more colorful. Narrow, bright green leaves tipped with yellow edges (which look pinkish in winter.) A fave with shrub fanciers.
- ❀ Sarcoxie: Also used everywhere, with shiny dark green leaves. Put the container up against a wall and you can train this one to climb.
- ❀ Wintercreeper (*Coloratus*): Green in summer, purple in winter, this will also train well up a wall. A dense grower, it may eventually outgrow its container.

❀ **Holly (*Ilex meserveae*):** If you hanker after the look of traditional holly, try varieties called Blue Princess or Blue Girl. They are hardy in cold climates, have lustrous blue-green leaves, and produce red berries in fall. In hot, dry locations, *Ilex cornuta* x *I rugosa* varieties such as China Girl may be a better bet.

❀ **Oregon grape (*Mahonia aquifolium*):** The name is misleading, as there nothing's "grapey" about this shrub. Instead, it resembles holly. It has similar shiny, prickly leaves, but is easier to grow than red-berried Christmas holly. Mahonia produces decorative bright yellow flowers in spring and blue berries later on. It doesn't mind some shade. Keep it in a sheltered area, away from cold winds.

❀ **Pieris (*Pieris japonica*):** A gorgeous shrub, but not for beginners because it requires an acid soil. Its container growing mix should be supplemented with lots of peat moss, acid humus (like chopped-up oak leaves), and a bit of garden sulphur (sold at garden centers). The Forest Flame variety is sensational. In spring, it sends out brilliant red foliage that turns green by summer.

Smart, simple, and inexpensive

If you like the minimalist Japanese style of landscaping (and don't have time to garden), group three conifers, of different heights, in plain green or gray pots. Surround them with a layer of gray pebbles. This looks contemporary, it won't cost much, and the only maintenance chore required is an occasional trim to keep the trees' shape.

Privacy screens

If you want to block out an undesirable view, the quickest way to do it is with container-grown shrubs. Position a group closely together in front of the area that you want to block out. Buy mature shrubs with dense vegetation. Some ideas:

❀ **Bamboo:** There are many types of bamboo, but the *Phyllostachys* varieties are most common. They grow vigorously, make great privacy screens, and are unlikely to get out of hand in containers. Their drawback in northern climates is that they must be brought indoors in the fall. Don't buy bamboo if you have limited indoor space. Before hauling indoors, prune them back hard.

❀ **Columnar cedar (*Thuja occidentalis* 'Holmstrup'):** Lovely emerald green foliage in a pyramid shape. A great screener, but it grows at a snail's pace. Buy large specimens.

❀ **Hick's upright yew (*Taxus media* 'Hicksii'):** Grows fast in acidic, sandy soil. Add peat moss or composted leaves to the growing mix (and, if possible, a bit of coarse builder's sand). Shape it by pruning in summer or early fall.

❀ **Japanese knotweed (*Polygonum cuspidatum*):** A shrubby "weed" with reddish, bamboo-like stems. Banished from most gardens because it's too invasive, but it often makes a great privacy screen in containers. Will grow virtually anywhere.

Large houseplants like *Ficus benjamina*, philodendron, and schefflera can also be pressed into service as privacy screens.

It's Worth Trying Trees

Don't let any garden center salesperson fool you. Persuading trees to flourish on a balcony or rooftop takes persistence. The majority of trees hate the wind and dry atmosphere up in the sky. An equally big deterrent is having their feet cramped into a container. Even the biggest planters don't provide sufficient space for the roots of most trees. Contrary to popular belief, tree roots don't extend downwards, in a fan shape. They ramble outwards, just below the surface of the soil, and after a few years, they may extend 30 ft./9 m from the tree's trunk. It's obviously tough to duplicate that kind of an environment in a planter. What usually happens is a container-grown tree will perform well for about three years, then, as it expands and runs out of rambling room, it will simply give up.

If you have your heart set on trees,

Do

✓ Research trees that grow in your area. Find someone who's already grown some on a balcony. Ask what worked.

✓ Seek out "dwarf" or "compact" varieties at garden centers. (Check labels carefully.)

✓ Plant trees in big—really big—planters, at least 2 ft./ 60 cm deep and as wide and long as you can make them. (Usually, the best option is to have some built.)

✓ In northern climates with long cold winters, use wooden beams several inches thick for planters, then line them with Styrofoam and plastic sheeting before filling with soil. Make sure there are drainage holes.

- ✓ Tell the garden center you want trees with compact root balls bound in burlap, rather than trees ready-planted in pots. (They'll be easier to carry.)
- ✓ Consider the height of the tree when it's being brought back from the garden center. (Will it fit into the elevator— or your car, if you're hauling it home yourself?)
- ✓ Use good growing mix (see page 33–34). Top it up every spring.
- ✓ Plant early in spring, when it's cool. Avoid planting when summer heat has hit.
- ✓ Tease out the roots with a small garden tool before planting.
- ✓ After planting, water every day in summer, without fail. Never let the tree dry out.
- ✓ Fertilize once a month until late summer. Then stop.
- ✓ Group trees together, for protection.
- ✓ Before winter freeze-up, water extra deeply. Then, if you can, provide some kind of protection (see page 135).

Good trees are expensive

Be wary of "bargains" sold off in the heat of the summer. If they are dried out, with dead branches or shriveling brown leaves, they probably aren't worth planting. Look for strong, healthy specimens with plenty of buds.

Don't

- ✗ Position trees where they'll bake in hot sunshine all day. Some afternoon shade is preferable.
- ✗ Prune container-grown trees too fiercely. Just snip off brown bits in spring. If it's a flowering tree, prune after the blooming period has finished.
- ✗ Bother with trees if you have dense shade. Most do require some sun to flourish.
- ✗ Dig up trees at a friend's place in the country and expect them to adapt well to growing in a container.

Seven deciduous trees that may work

Generally speaking, shrubby trees adapt better to container growing than those with tall slender trunks. Trees with a weeping habit (i.e., their branches cascade downwards, instead of reaching outwards or upwards) are also a good choice on balconies, where you have another balcony floor directly above yours. Try:

❀ **Amur maple (*Acer ginnala*):** Grown in the ground, this can be a rampaging nuisance. Confined to a container, however, this tough, bushy type of maple sometimes performs admirably. It can reach 20 ft./6 m high, but seldom does in a planter. Several amur maples in a row make a good privacy screen for a large terrace, courtyard, or rooftop. They turn brilliant red in fall.

❀ **Crabapple *(Malus)*:** There are over 800 varieties of crabapples and most grow too big for containers. But try a weeping variety called Red Jade. It grows only about 10 ft./3 m high and produces deep pink or red flowers in spring and gorgeous fruit (which look like bunches of cherries) in fall. The hanging branches are graceful throughout the summer.

❀ **Dogwoods (*Cornus*):** Strictly speaking, dogwoods are shrubs, but some grow tall enough to be considered trees. Try Bud's Yellow, which has a bushy, rounded shape with long yellow twiggy branches, or Silver Leaf (*C. alba elegantissima*), which has pretty green foliage with white edges, plus lovely crimson branches in winter. They can grow about 8 ft./2.5 m tall, but probably won't in containers.

❀ **Dwarf Korean lilac (*Syringa meyeri* 'Palibin' [*velutina*]):** This has pretty lavender pink flowers and can grow about 6.5 ft./2 m tall. It looks striking in a container. Needs full sun. Prune dead flower heads off, right after they finish blooming, or you won't get lots of flowers the following year. Be sure to ask for the "standard" (or tree) variety, rather than the shrub version.

❀ **Japanese maple (*Acer palmatum*):** Graceful trees—currently hot with gardeners—that have arching branches and delicate foliage in red, golden red, green, or purple.

With plenty of mulch and moisture, they can do well in containers. They prefer a bit of shade in the afternoon. Weeping varieties like Crimson Queen are best for small spaces.

❀ **Weeping birch (*Betula pendula*):** Birches tend to succumb to bugs and diseases, but some balcony gardeners have success with this type. It has fine, dark green foliage and, in perfect conditions, can reach about 15 ft./4.5 m high. If you buy a top-grafted variety (ask at the garden center), it can be kept to half that size. On a rooftop, clump birches are also a possibility, because they're less inclined to topple over than their cousins, which have slender trunks.

❀ **Weeping pea shrub (*Caragana arborescens* 'Pendula'):** This gets the thumbs up from many balcony gardeners. It copes admirably with city pollution, produces yellow flowers in late spring, and its cascading, bright green leaves look pretty in planters. It grows from 3 to 6.5 ft./1 to 2 m tall. Another weeping pea shrub, *Caragana arborescens* 'Walker', is less dependable but may work in some locations.

Evergreens to experiment with

Evergreens (also called conifers) are often recommended to gardeners on the grounds that they supply welcome greenery all year round (unlike the deciduous trees listed above). In reality, however, you won't see much of your evergreen trees in a northern climate during the winter, because most need to be swaddled in burlap or plastic netting in fall to stop heavy snow breaking their branches (see page 135).

Container-grown upright evergreens are actually at their best in summertime, when their lush new growth provides a pleasing backdrop to other plants on balconies. Try:

❀ **Cedars (*Thuja occidentalis*):** Slow-growing varieties, with columnar shapes, are best for containers. Balcony gardeners report success with De Groot's Spire (very narrow, a good accent tree) and Holmstrup (a wonderful emerald green pyramid). Both may reach 10 ft./3 m high.

Cut dead brown bits off in spring. If you prefer a cedar with a rounded shape, try a compact "globe" variety. There are many on the market.

⚘ **Euonymus**: Shrub forms of euonymus are hugely popular (see pages 99–100) because they're so tough and easy to grow. Thanks to tinkering by experts, you can also now find varieties grown as trees. Try *Euonymus alata* 'Compacta' (be sure to ask for the tree form), which has spectacular red foliage in fall. Its odd zigzagging branches can also be beautiful in winter. Coated in ice, with the sun behind them, they look like stained glass.

Hot tip

"Position a tree near a window during the winter and hang a birdfeeder in it. I spend hours watching birds come to my weeping peashrub."
—*Wendy Humphries, balcony gardener*

⚘ **Firs (*Abies*):** Firs are iffy in containers. If you want one, try a dwarf balsam variety like *Abies balsamea* 'Nana'.

⚘ **Pines (*Pinus*):** Mugo pines are a fave with many gardeners—and indeed they are fun, with mounded shapes and big, spiky needles. Pick a dwarf variety and don't be afraid to keep pruning new growth back to keep the nice shape. Also worth trying is a native Scots pine (*Pinus strobus*) called White Mountain, from the mountains of New Hampshire. Avoid Austrian pine (*Pinus nigra*). Its needles are too open and spindly in containers.

⚘ **Spruces (*Picea*):** Skip spruces that grow enormous. Pick a tough, native variety if you have long cold winters. Good bets in cold areas: white North American spruce (*Picea glauca*), which has a pyramid shape, and blue spruce (*Picea pungens*) in compact varieties called Hoopsi Blue, Kosters, or Moerheim. They have pretty blue or silver-blue needles.

⚘ **Yews (*Taxus*):** If you have a ground-floor courtyard with absolutely no sun, try yews. They're the only evergreens that will tolerate complete shade. Generally tough, they also don't sulk in city pollution. Varieties like Hicks or Upright Japanese look good on either side of a door. Spreading varieties like Dense or Runyan are good for flowerbeds, but need to be pruned to keep their shape. Many yews are slow growing (be patient!). In shade, don't bother with the new so-called golden varieties. (These need sun for the colors to develop properly, and the green-leaved yews look more fetching anyway.)

A taste of topiary

Disliked for many years, trees trimmed into topiary shapes are back in fashion. They make striking accents on balconies and are also easy, because someone else does all the barbering in advance. Buy an evergreen—cedar, spruce, juniper —that's already been trained into a "pom pom," or "poodle," topiary design. Then simply keep on giving the tree a light haircut to keep its shape.

Be warned, however, that evergreens turned into topiary are expensive. (Understandably so. It often takes years for tree nurseries to fashion plants into those fascinating twists, twirls, and mounds.) Also, topiary tends to be short lived in containers. Stick to regular trees if you're on a tight budget.

The Instant Garden:
For People with No Time

Mother Nature is bountiful, but she doesn't like to be rushed. That can be both a benefit and a drawback when you're gardening on a balcony (or in any kind of small space). Waiting for plants to develop and flowers to start blooming teaches us two great virtues: patience and humility. It's also relaxing. The more we garden, the more we become aware of the rhythm of the seasons—and of the fact that human beings can't control everything.

However, when opportunities to introduce flowers and foliage are limited, the pace of nature can be mighty frustrating. Many annuals don't start putting on a show until late in the summer. Perennials sometimes take years before strutting their stuff properly, as do some shrubs. That's fine in a garden around a house, where there's usually something else green (like a lawn and trees) to provide an outdoorsy feeling in the meantime. But what about when you're stuck with a bare, boring balcony or courtyard surrounded by concrete?

The solution is to buy big pre-started plants instead of small ones. Most annual flowers are sold at garden centers in plastic cell paks, four or six plants to a pak. Instead of choosing these diminutive specimens, look for individual plants in plastic or fiber pots at least 4 in./10 cm wide. They aren't hard to find nowadays. Follow the same routine with perennials and shrubs. Go for gallon- rather than pint-sized. Then put those in your containers instead. They'll produce results quicker.

Start with spring-flowering plants. Use them for a couple of months. Then, once their flowers are finished (or start to look less than their best), remove those plants and buy some replacements that will bloom throughout summer. When fall's coming, move on to plants that will provide a splash in late summer and fall. Finally, select some evergreens to brighten up the balcony in winter. An instant garden is that simple.

Drawbacks to hurry-up gardening

The "instant" style of growing things is undeniably easy, but it's not all a bed of roses. First, there's the cost: bigger plants are more expensive. Second, the hurry-up plants probably won't survive long, for two reasons: they were probably pampered in perfect conditions in greenhouses (and your balcony, rooftop, or courtyard won't provide the same environment), and if you transplant them, bigger plants, especially annuals, go through more shock than small ones. Third, it's wasteful. You wind up throwing a lot of plant material out, because you keep changing the display throughout the growing season. (Be kind to the environment; look for a friend with a compost heap where you can dump the discards instead of putting them in the garbage.)

That said, if you simply want a quick, colorful show, have limited space to grow things, and aren't particularly interested in the rituals of gardening, the quick, no nurturing method works well.

The best way to do it

Any kind of container can be used for an instant garden, but the easiest is a window box or big planter. Select a deep one, line it with plastic sheeting (sold at hardware stores; big garbage bags also work fine), then spread a layer of peat moss on the bottom of the box. Make sure there's a drainage hole.

Look for established, healthy plants with big flower heads. Nestle them, still in their original plastic pots, inside the window box or planter. (It's not necessary to transplant them if the pots are a fair size.) Cram in as many as you can. Change the pot groupings with the seasons. Keep them moist. You can grow all kinds of plants, annual and perennial, in this fashion.

Some plant suggestions

In spring

In sun or part shade: Start off with spring-flowering bulbs: narcissus, tulips, hyacinths. When they fade, swap them for pansies, primulas, *Arabis* (commonly known as rock cress), *Aurinia saxatile* (often called Cloth of Gold), lobelia (trailing varieties).

In summer

In sun: Petunias, geraniums (which will need big individual pots), bidens, gazanias, Dusty Miller, marigolds, salvias, trailing plants like periwinkle *Vinca major* and *Helichrysum* 'Spike', fountain grass (*Pennisetum alopecuroides*) and purple fountain grass (*P. setaceum* 'Rubrum').

In shade or part shade: Begonias, nicotiana, hardy geraniums, periwinkle *Vinca major*, houseplants like *dracaena* and Chinese evergreens. (Bring yours outside: see pages 49–51.)

In fall

In sun, part shade, or shade: Ornamental kales and cabbages in pinks, greens, and yellows; Icicle pansies; periwinkle *Vinca major*; miniature pumpkins and a hot new decorative item, osage oranges (get them at florists and garden centres), impaled on bamboo skewers, for accents.

In winter

Miniature conifers (spruces, cedars, junipers, cypresses), trailing varieties of euonymus (see pages 99–100); twigs of corkscrew hazel and bright red dogwood (sold at florists) for height; miniature outdoor lights twined around branches, if you have an electrical outlet on the balcony.

Turn to urns

The instant treatment outlined above also works well, on a smaller scale, in urns. Fashionable among many gardeners, these classic containers are an inspired choice if you like a formal, elegant style. They're available in clay, copper, and concrete, but come in lightweight resin too, which is preferable, as it's easy to move around. Go for metal if your balcony is very windy. Avoid clay and concrete if you want to leave the urns outside all winter.

Do

✓ Position a single urn front and center, where it's visible from indoors, if your space is small.

✓ Remove plants from their plastic or fiber pots and transplant them into the urns. Don't try cramming pots in. There won't be enough space.

✓ Pack plants tightly together. You'll be replacing this collection with something else soon, so they don't need room to expand.

✓ Cut sides of fiber pots open with a knife when plants won't come out easily.

✓ Use a knife to make slashes into the sides of big plant root balls before planting. It won't hurt the plants and helps them settle in.

✓ Pour in packaged potting soil, but don't fill the urn so it's overflowing. Dirt dribbling down the sides isn't pretty.

Don't

✗ Work on a new instant arrangement after soil freezes in fall and winter. Soil that isn't frozen is essential. If you have no time to plant before frost hits, remove 5 in./ 13 cm of soil and store it indoors until you're ready.

> ### Hot tip
> "Avoid using florists' oasis to position plants and branches in containers. It flies out during windy weather. Tuck them firmly into the soil instead."
> —Ann Dobec, garden designer

Mums aren't the word

Potted mums (botanical name Chrysanthemum *or* Dendranthema*) are cheap in the fall. They come in wonderful colors—yellows, russets, purples—and pots of them look great on a balcony. But once mums get nipped by the frost, their flower edges go brown and look lousy. Don't mix mums in with other fall arrangements. Use them on their own. Ornamental kales and cabbages are more economical because they last longer.*

Difficult Sites: How to Transform Them

Some balconies, terraces, courtyards, and rooftops seem like disaster areas where nothing will grow. However, with a few cunning moves, you can persuade Mother Nature to cooperate. Here are some ideas for transforming inhospitable spaces:

The windy, cold balcony

Often found high in the sky, on the north sides of high-rises. It gets no direct sun, feels freezing cold most of the time, and is constantly buffeted by winds.

Solution: Skip flowers and deciduous greenery. Go for a minimalist look with two hardy conifers, an arrangement of gray pebbles, and a stone statue or interesting large rock. Use heavy planters in stone or wood (covered with copper sheeting). Put rocks in the bottom of planters to weigh them down, then add plain potting soil. (Don't use lightweight growing mixes containing vermiculite. It will blow out.) Position the display where it's visible from indoors. Conifers to consider: junipers (*J. horizontalis* 'Compact Andorra' and *J. chinensis* 'Golden Pfitzer'), native white spruce (*Picea glauca*), and Siberian cypress (*Microbiota decussata*).

The dark, damp courtyard

Usually at the back or sides of townhouses. It's small, surrounded by high walls or fences, never gets sun, and is gloomy all day.

Solution: Lighten things up. Paint surrounding walls or fences white (if that's permitted). Add a small white table and chairs—and plastic planters, which you paint in white or hot hues (yellow, orange, fire engine red). Include a trellis on one wall, or a pottery "sun" that picks up the colors of your pots. Avoid sun-loving flowers. Grow evergreens and light-leaved foliage plants that survive in shade. Try columnar Hicks yews, climbing wintercreeper (*Euonymus fortunei* 'Coloratus' or *E. fortunei* 'Sarcoxie'), and potted white caladiums and coleus. In flowerbeds, try *E. fortunei* 'Emerald Gaiety', shrubby Oregon grape (*Mahonia aquifolium*), periwinkle *Vinca minor*, deadnettle (*Lamium maculatum),* hostas, and that old garden standby, impatiens.

The fried egg balcony (or rooftop)

All too common. Usually faces south, on tops or sides of buildings. Hot, exposed, and windy, so plants keep drying out.

Solution: Put up windbreaks. (Cheap bamboo blinds, turned on their sides, can be effective.) Install a water feature, if possible. A small pond or a trickling fountain will make it seem instantly cooler. Grow drought-tolerant plants: yarrows (*Achillea*), milkweed (*Asclepias tuberosa*), portulaca, daylilies (*Hemerocallis*), Cloth of Gold *(Aurinia saxatile)*, gaillardias, gazanias, Russian sage (*Perovskia atriplicifolia*), sedums, snow-in-summer (*Cerastium tomentosum*), and ornamental grasses (pick dwarf varieties, such as fountain grass, *Pennisetum alopecuroides* 'Hameln'; tall varieties will probably get flattened in winds).

> **Hot tip**
>
> "Be proud of your new gardening endeavor, whatever it is. Don't refer to it as 'just a balcony.' It sounds unimportant. This is your garden—and that's what you should call it."
> —*Denis Flanagan, gardening show host*

Conserve moisture in your containers by putting a "living mulch" of herbs around the base of shrubs and flowers. Lemon thyme, woolly thyme, oregano, and savory work well. Put containers on castors so you can wheel them out of hot sunshine into the shade.

When all else fails, try a new craze: trough gardening with alpine plants. Fill troughs (low-sided containers) with a mix of one part compost, one part potting soil, and one part coarse, gritty sand. Add some crushed slag on top. (Buy the latter two at builders' yards.) Super-tough plants to try: hens and chicks (*Sempervivum*), sea pinks (*Armeria maritima*), saxifrages, low-growing sedums, lemon thyme, woolly thyme, and donkey tail spurge (*Euphorbia myrsinites*). The troughs can be left outside over the winter.

The concrete bunker balcony

Usually set deep into the sides of buildings. Has a low ceiling, three solid walls, and another half-wall of concrete, facing the outside. Dark and gloomy.

Solution: Paint the balcony ceiling white. (Use a paint roller. *Don't* climb up a ladder if you live in a high-rise.) Raise plants off the balcony floor, close to the light source, in window boxes or hanging baskets. Buy containers and outdoor furniture in light colors. Hang a mirror on one wall, and a light-colored piece of art on the wall opposite. Don't clutter the place up. Go for flower and foliage plants in white and warm colors that will tolerate some shade. Try begonias, browallia, mimulus, torenia, snapdragons, white caladiums, and coleus in reds, oranges, and golds. Offset the flowers with trailing plants like periwinkle *Vinca major* 'Variegata' and sweet potato vine Blackie or Limelight.

The truly tiny balcony (or deck)

There's barely space for even a chair, and it's often surrounded by a high railing, blocking most of the view.

Solution: Buy a folding patio chair that you can stash indoors. Hang a half-basket from the railing, facing into your unit. Fill it with small flowering annuals, particularly trailing varieties. In sun: regal or ivy geraniums, mini petunias, Swan River daisies (*Brachyscome*), licorice vine (*Helichrysum petiolare*). In shade: small trailing begonias, browallia, fuchsias, scented geraniums, nicotiana, sweet potato vine Blackie, coleus with small leaves, periwinkle *Vinca major* 'Variegata'. See if there's space for a mini-trellis on either side of the balcony door. Grow easy-to-grow annual vines up it (see pages 94–95). Look for triangular containers that can be tucked into corners of the balcony.

Grow a bit of grass

If you love lawns, here's an inexpensive way to have a tiny one: buy a big tray (or ask at a garden center for a shallow wooden planting flat) and line it with plastic. Punch some drainage holes. Lay a piece of sod in the tray. Water regularly and trim with scissors. It won't last more than one summer—and you need a very sunny location—but it will give you a nice, green taste of turf.

The non-existent balcony

Nothing more than a concrete ledge, with a window or sliding screen door opening on to it. Usually has a high railing.

Solution: Hang a half-basket from the railing and fill it with flowers (see above). Underneath it, if there's room, place a long window box filled with eye-catching upright annuals: zonal geraniums in red or shocking pink, salvias in several shades, snapdragons, a purple foliage plant, *Perilla frutescens.* Or go minimalist with three narrow, columnar evergreens in individual containers. Try cedar *Thuja occidentalis* 'De Groot's Spire', or juniper *Juniperus virginiana* 'Blue Arrow'. If the window opening on to the ledge isn't tall, try a container of hens and chicks (*Sempervivum*). They're tough-as-nails plants that you can leave to fend for themselves year-round.

When Gardening Is a Pain

Growing things is good for us. Experts have found that gardening can produce endorphin "highs" similar to those experienced by joggers. Simply looking at greenery has been proven to reduce stress, lower blood pressure, and relieve muscle tension. Alzheimer's patients do much better in residences with gardens than in those with nowhere to get a taste of the great outdoors. In fact, there are so many remarkable benefits to being around plants—and taking care of them—horticultural therapy is a growing field. It's being used to successfully treat patients with a variety of mental and physical problems.

That said, gardening can also be a pain in the neck. And the back. And the knees. And the wrists. The list goes on. The older and creakier we get, the harder it is to handle those activities associated with gardening: bending down, digging, lifting heavy plants and pots. According to condo developers, the main reason why many older couples decide to quit the family home is that they don't want to get aching backs maintaining the front and back yard anymore.

However, if you've gardened all your life, it's often hard to give it up. That's why, for many people, a balcony or courtyard garden proves to be such a plus. It keeps us connected with nature, yet is small and manageable. There's no lawn to cut, no big flowerbeds to weed and fuss over. You can grow a bit of this and a bit of that, and not feel overpowered.

How to avoid sore joints

If you have arthritis or other mobility problems, here are ways to ensure that gardening is a pleasure, not a pain:

Do

✓ Keep gardening projects small. Just one flowerpot is enough for some people.

✓ Get rid of heavy metal tools. Plastic trowels and watering cans are easier to handle.

✓ Paint tools yellow, so you can spot them easily. (Many manufacturers now sensibly produce tools in this color.)

✓ Hang a basket at waist height, on a balcony railing or wall. Store tools in it.

✓ Garden in raised containers. Window boxes attached to balcony railings work well if you can stand up. If you prefer to sit—or are in a wheelchair—get a sturdy wooden bench built 2 ft./60 cm off the ground, and put flowerpots on it. Make the bench wide enough so your knees can slide underneath it comfortably.

✓ Always have a stool or chair close by so you can take a rest.

✓ Use lightweight resin containers (see page 28) and soil-less mix (see page 33).

Don't

✗ Bend down to do anything. Sweep up garden debris with a long-handled broom and dustpan. Grow plants vertically (see pages 90–95).

✗ Put containers in places where you have to stretch to reach them.

✗ Garden in the hot midday sun. Always wear a hat.

✗ Buy "difficult" plants. Stick to kinds that are easy to grow. Planting things that will cause you stress defeats the whole purpose of gardening.

Don't haul stones upstairs

Cheap lightweight sponges, sold at dollar stores, are excellent as drainage in the bottom of containers. Buy a package of them. They're easier and lighter than bits of crockery or stones.

Tools to try if you ache

Stiff joints or sore back? Buy "enabling" tools. Some mail order garden product companies, aware that Boomers are getting older and creakier, sell them. (Look in gardening magazines.) Among the options are:

❀ **Ergonomic hoes, trowels, and cultivators:** Often weird-looking (shaped like bicycle handlebars with pistol grips), they're designed to keep hands and wrists in a natural position while you dig. Rheumatologists recommend them.

❀ **Telescoping tools:** Made of lightweight aluminum with cushioned handles. Usually hoes, rakes, and brooms.

❀ **Kneeler benches:** Sold in many garden centers, they have cushioned kneeling pads and handles. (But on a balcony, gardening in raised containers is your best bet.)

Hot tip

"Wrap tools like scissors and pruners in thin pieces of foam rubber to cushion joints—and wear cotton gloves."
—Karen York, horticultural therapist

❋ **Wrist wraps:** Like the protectors worn by roller bladers. They make wielding a trowel easier.

❋ **Long-handled picker-uppers:** Make it possible to lift things from the floor without bending over.

Safety in the Sky

It can be downright dangerous gardening on a balcony—especially if you're high in the sky. Most condominium and apartment buildings now have regulations stipulating what gardeners can and can't do. Often these prohibitions can seem unnecessary, but they are usually introduced for safety reasons.

How to avoid accidents

Do

✓ Hang window boxes inside the balcony.

✓ Buy sturdy, well-made supports for the boxes. (Cheap ones are often absurdly flimsy.) They should attach to both the balcony railing and the window box with long screws.

✓ Take careful measurements before going out to buy boxes and supports. Get a professional to install them if you aren't sure how to do the job yourself.

✓ Make sure the wires of hanging baskets are heavy enough to cope with strong winds. Attach these wires firmly to the baskets and to hooks, not nails, screwed into the balcony ceiling, using concrete plugs. (Or put up brackets on balcony walls.)

✓ Wrap lengths of wire completely around hanging baskets and run them to hooks on balcony side walls.

✓ If you aren't sure what your balcony ceiling and walls are made of (and what type of screws to use), ask the building management for guidance.

✓ Buy safety straps that go around wrists for pruners and scissors. It's all too easy to drop tools over the edge.

✓ Use a watering wand to reach pots.

Don't

✗ Place any containers on concrete ledges of balconies.

✗ Suspend baskets so high up you need to climb on to a chair to water them or tidy up plants.

✗ Buy hanging baskets that are bigger than 15 in./40 cm in diameter. Also avoid ready-planted ones with flimsy plastic hangers that aren't strong enough to support baskets filled with wet soil and plants.

✗ Let climbing plants ramble all over the place, so you have to lean far over the balcony edge to prune.

Be a happy hooker

Not a hazardous one. All kinds of ingenious hooks are available that will stop hanging plants from crashing to the ground. Look for these at garden centers and home renovation stores and always follow the manufacturers' instructions.

❀ **Ceiling hooks:** Cup hooks, often with a screw attached, or a toggle bolt (a winged bit for fastening into hollow ceilings).

❀ **Swivel hooks:** Rotate so that the plant can be turned to get sun on all sides.

❀ **Hanging container brackets:** Usually L-shaped or resembling decorative scrolls, for fastening into walls. The best ones are made from a heavy metal, such as wrought iron. (Avoid cheap, lightweight aluminum ones.) Some have pulleys attached so you can raise and lower hanging baskets.

❀ **Planter brackets:** They have solid metal arms that hook over balcony railings or screw into walls. The best ones are adjustable: there's a sliding section that expands or contracts to accommodate the width of both the balcony railing and planters. Smaller brackets are available for individual pots.

> ## Hot tip
> "Build a simple wooden work bench, with a window box on top. Store messy gardening stuff underneath the bench, hidden by some short, dark green curtains. It's easier to garden safely if you keep things tidy."
> —*Dave Wilson, high-rise balcony gardener*

Bugs (Blech!): Ways to Banish The

One big advantage to growing things in containers on balconies is less bugs and diseases. Insects and creepy-crawlies mostly multiply down at ground level, in the soil, and don't tend to travel too high up. The same can be said of soil-borne infections and diseases. People with regular gardens down on terra firma have to cope with many more problems in this department than do balcony gardeners.

That said, your pots and planters are unlikely to be sitting pretty, unblemished and unbothered, all the time. Mother Nature is actually a bit of a sadist. She likes to ensure that we endure a bit of pain along with all that pleasure that her offspring give us. Sooner or later, all gardens, irrespective of their location, are likely to get visited by something vile and annoying.

In the live critter department, be on the watch for SEAS of problems—that is, slugs, earwigs, aphids, and scale. Where plant diseases are concerned, watch out mostly for downy mildew.

Slugs

If you're being bugged by slugs, chances are it's rained a lot recently, or you've overwatered your plants. Slugs love it damp. To get rid of them,

Do

✓ Try beer. Yes, it does kill slugs. But this precious liquid costs so much nowadays, why treat the slimeballs to a blissful, boozy end? Here's a cheaper alternative: mix two tablespoons of brewer's yeast (sold at health food stores) with a teaspoon of sugar in a 16 oz./500 ml yogurt container of water. Pour the concoction into beer traps sunk in the ground to soil level. Use old saucers, empty sardine cans, or ready-made traps with lids (pretty ones are sold everywhere). Slugs drink themselves silly, fall in, and drown. Replace when it rains.

✓ Use copper tape—a good choice for container gardeners. Wrap a strip of this tape around the outside of each pot. Slugs don't like crawling across it. Copper tape is sold at some garden centers (one brand is called SureFire Slug and Snail Copper Barrier), but it's unfortunately pricey. Also, once the tape gets dirty, the nocturnal nuisances tend to come back—and it won't deter slugs already inside the pot, lurking under the soil.

✓ Try diatomaceous earth. Sold at garden centers, this is made from the ground-up skeletons of sea crustaceans. Touted as environmentally friendly, it kill slugs by puncturing holes in their sides (but unfortunately does the same to bees). Pour a pile of the razor-sharp crystals into the toe of old panty hose (or two layers of cheesecloth), tie a knot, then hit your plants with this weapon, coating all the stems, flowers, and foliage with dust (paying particular attention to the undersides of leaves). Repeat after rain.

✓ Enlist Fido's help. Some people say encircling affected plants with dog (or human) hair keeps slugs away. So does a ring of ash (from cigarettes or wood fires), diatomaceous earth, crunched up egg shells, or salt.

✓ Dig into planters in spring and look for slug eggs. They resemble tiny pearls, laid in clusters. You can easily pick them out.

✓ Go out at night with a flashlight and handpick slugs. (Be brave, they *are* horribly slimy.) Drop into a cupful of salty water. Or, if you're squeamish, mix up a plastic sprayer of water with a teaspoon of ammonia added. Spray directly onto slugs. Make sure the critters die. Squirt twice, if necessary. They can be remarkably tenacious.

✓ Remove the lower leaves of plants, so slugs don't have any damp hiding places. Check regularly underneath pots and in cracks between paving stones.

✓ Be careful of commercial slug baits. Always read labels. The ones containing metaldehyde can cause kidney damage in pets and kids. Varieties containing iron phosphate are less harmful.

Don't

✗ Grow green, leafy plants. Slugs love hostas, nasturtiums, basil, and veggies like Swiss chard and lettuce. They hate hard-leaved plants like rhododendrons. If you must have hostas, look for slug-resistant varieties. Among them are Abiqua Drinking Gourd, Invincible, Serendipity, and Sum and Substance.

✗ Ignore slugs. They're voracious varmints. Even a couple can reduce a pretty plant to shreds in next to no time.

Earwigs

Earwigs are hard-shelled insects, about half an inch (1.25 cm) long, with pincers. Horror stories (mostly exaggerated) abound about them. However, these creepy-looking invaders can actually be beneficial in gardens because they munch on another annoying critter, the aphid.

That said, don't endure earwigs if great mobs of them are chewing and destroying your plants. You can find out if these pincered pests are the problem by checking at night with a flashlight. Plants sometimes crawl with earwigs. Some remedies:

❀ Earwigs like to congregate in damp, dark spaces. Put some old garden hose 6 in./15 cm long around plants that are getting attacked. Every morning, dunk these lengths into a pail of soapy water. The drowned (you hope) denizens should fall out.

❀ Leave scrunched up balls of wet newspapers around plants. Do the same as above.

❀ Get some empty containers with steep sides: tin cans, margarine tubs, yogurt containers. Pour in one tablespoon each of vegetable oil, soy sauce, and molasses. Place containers next to plants where earwigs are munching. Bend a couple of leaves over the cans to stimulate earwiggy interest (but make sure that once the bugs topple in, they can't crawl out). Leave overnight. Check next morning. Some gardeners report huge hauls of dead earwigs with this concoction.

🌺 Avoid the chemical antidotes to earwigs that are on the market—they tend to be toxic.

Aphids

The trouble with aphids is that you usually can't see the damn things. They're flying insects, but most are microscopic. That doesn't stop them being big-time nuisances, however. Aphids suck juices from the stems and leaves of all kinds of flowers. If a plant is under attack, it may wilt and appear pale (or even yellow), with curled or stunted leaves and flower heads. Pull up a leaf and look underneath: if it's puckered, aphids are probably to blame. To get rid of them,

🌺 Spray with soapy water three times, at three-day intervals. Pay the most attention to the undersides of leaves.

🌺 Mix a plastic sprayer full of a semi-environmentally friendly insecticide called pyrethrum (sold pre-mixed at garden centers) with a tablespoon of isopropryl alcohol (from hardware stores). Spray directly on aphids.

- Blast aphids off plants with a garden hose (but be careful of the neighbors.)
- Put up yellow sticky traps next to plants.
- Welcome ladybugs to your balcony. They eat hundreds of aphids a day. (You can buy these Florence Nightingales of the garden by mail order from environmentally friendly pest control companies.)

Dish soap works fine

Commercial insecticidal soaps are expensive. You can get the same results by mixing up a few squirts of a mild dish soap (not detergent) into a plastic sprayer of water. Start treating plants early, the moment you see bugs. Spray everything, including the undersides of leaves. With serious infestations, dunk the entire plant, pot and all, into a bucket of soapy water.

Scale

Scale isn't crud found inside the kettle. It's alive—a horrid insect with a hard, horny casing that sucks sap from stems. If there's a sticky substance dripping underneath your plants and their leaves are yellow and dropping, the problem is probably scale. Many popular plants like euonymus, geraniums, peonies, and canna lilies get attacked by scale. Serious infestations may mean throwing the plant out. To limit scale,

- Scrape the limpet-like casings off stems with the back of a knife, then spray with soapy water.
- Dab insects with a Q-tip dipped in isopropryl alcohol.
- Douse the entire plant in a horticultural spray that contains oil. Before spraying, cut off any stems that are heavily infected.

The matter of mildew

Plant diseases are blessedly few on balconies, provided you buy healthy plants and sterilized growing mix. However, in humid climates, downy mildew can show up. A grayish or white mold may appear on stems, leaves, and flower heads. Eventually, the whole plant gets limp, distorted, and ugly. Once established, mildew is difficult to eradicate. To avoid outbreaks,

Do

✓ Position pots in areas with good air circulation.
✓ Leave plenty of space between plants.
✓ Water early on sunny days.
✓ The moment you detect even a wisp of mildew, fill a plastic sprayer with water, mixed with a tablespoon of baking soda. Douse the plant three times, at three-day intervals.

Don't

✗ Use icy water, straight from the faucet. Let it sit in a watering can for a while.
✗ Wet leaves when watering plants.
✗ Water at night.
✗ Overwater.

> ## Hot tip
> "I object to making up complicated concoctions to kill slugs. A simple and effective remedy is to pour hot water over stems of wormwood (*Artemisia absinthium*). Discard stems, let the water cool, then spray or pour on plants."
> —*Dominique Leonard, perennials fan*

Those Annoying Garden Gatecrashers

They drop by uninvited. They dig up, eat, maim, and destroy plants. They often leave souvenirs of their visits behind. Here's how to cope with unwelcome interlopers from the animal kingdom.

Pigeons and starlings

Seldom a problem for ground-level gardeners, but people in condos and apartments are often driven crazy by these crappy, persistent high fliers. Deterrents to try:

❀ Stretch narrow mesh black plastic netting (sold at garden centers) over the entire balcony opening. Attach it to side walls, ceiling, and the half-wall facing outside, using strips

of furring and screws. This shut-out approach may sound drastic, but it's worth the effort, according to some pigeon-plagued balcony gardeners. The netting is barely visible and it doesn't block the view, but the birds are stopped in their tracks. Note: this will only work, of course, on an enclosed type of balcony, with solid side walls.

❋ Pull out a kid's wire Slinky toy along the concrete ledge of a balcony. Add some hooks to keep it in place. Or try a length of shiny plastic string attached to the balcony walls and stretched along the ledge. Positioned two or three inches above the ledge, it may deter birds from landing.

❋ Aluminum pie pans, or strips of fluorescent tape flapping about. (These may bother your neighbors more than the pigeons.)

❋ An artificial owl, sitting on the balcony railing, sometimes works. Often doesn't. The best kind have moving heads that bob and turn in air currents. They're scarier to pigeons and starlings. (But if you can entice some real live hawks to make a nest close by, that will work far better.)

Cats

Love 'em or hate 'em, felines find their way into courtyard gardens and, sometimes, onto balconies and rooftops. If you want to stop pussies prowling around,

Do

✓ Try growing an annual called *Coleus canina*. It has a strong smell (particularly when it dries out) that repels cats. You can find it at garden centers, often sold under the name Scardy Cat. Plant several of them among your other plants.

✓ Stick bamboo barbecue skewers, close together, in all your containers. Cats don't take kindly to their sharp, pointed ends.

Don't

✗ Use blood meal or fish emulsion as a fertilizer. Cats are drawn to the smell of both—and will dig up soil in search of a snack.

✗ Plant a fashionable blue-flowered perennial called *Nepeta faassenii*. Its common name is catmint or catnip. (Enough said.)
✗ Put up a bird feeder. It will attract feathered friends *and* their predators.

Squirrels

The bushy-tailed brigade come in several colors—gray, red, black. Whatever their uniform, they can all be a colossal nuisance, particularly in ground-level gardens. Tips:

Do

✓ Smooth out areas where you've planted things. Squirrels often dig in disturbed soil in search of edibles such as nuts.
✓ Try the bamboo skewer routine (see under "Cats," on page 129).
✓ Spray plants with a garlic and water solution. Repeat after it rains. But don't use cayenne pepper or mothballs. (Pepper can blind squirrels and cause them incredible pain. Mothballs are toxic to pets and kids. Animal protection societies now frown upon these two deterrents.)

Don't

✗ Grow tulips if your area is infested with squirrels. They will dig up bulbs, break off flower heads, nibble on petals—often right in front of you. Daffodils or other kinds of narcissus are a better bet. (They are poisonous to squirrels.)
✗ Add bone meal to growing mix. It attracts squirrels. Commercial fertilizers high in phosphorus (the middle number on packages, for instance, 10-20-10) are a better bet.
✗ Don't hang up a bird feeder. Squirrels love snacking on all those seedy selections too.

Raccoons, skunks, and foxes

These so-called wild animals are no longer restricted to the wild. They're often found in populated areas, because the pickings are better. (In fact, raccoons are far bigger and healthier in cities nowadays than in the country.) To help deal with them,

Hot tip

"Get a dog. I let mine out on the balcony any time pigeons drop by. That scares them off."
—*Wendy Humphries, balcony gardener*

❁ Store garbage in sealed containers, kept firmly closed with bungee cords.

❁ Don't have a water garden. Raccoons love rummaging around in ponds in search of fish. They will also wash other food they find in pond water—and make a dreadful mess.

❁ Buy a motion-activated sprinkler. It has a highly sensitive infrared sensor that sprays a jet of water when it detects any movement. Many gardeners say this works like a charm at scaring off nocturnal visitors (dogs and cats too).

❁ Leave lights on, or play a radio, all night outside (but check with the neighbors first).

When Winter Comes: Survival Strategies

A balcony or rooftop garden is fine and dandy in summertime, but what about the winter? Probably the biggest drawback to growing things in containers is those dreary, freezing months, in all their guises. Many trees, shrubs, and perennials that do perfectly well planted in the ground can turn temperamental in pots and planters once Jack Frost arrives. Often the severity of the temperature isn't the problem. What affects plants far more is the thermometer going up and down like a yo-yo throughout the winter. This kind of weather is affecting more and more regions of North America; the supposedly cold season has stopped being consistently cold. There's snow one day, then it's rainy and warm the next. When that happens, plants get as confused as humans do. They may start to sprout during the thaw, then their tender buds and burgeoning roots get whomped by winter all over again. No wonder they give up.

Container-grown plants actually survive winter best in areas where heavy snow comes early, then stays on the ground. The white stuff acts as a protective blanket, maintaining plants at much the same temperature for months on end. In areas where that doesn't happen, where there's not enough snow and no constancy to the temperature, even plants that are supposedly hardy in your region may not be able to cope.

Shop wisely

When buying plants for an urban gardener, bear this mind: they'll have a better chance of survival if you pick perennials, shrubs, and trees that are hardy in areas *two zones colder* than yours. For instance, if you garden in Zone 6, select plants that are hardy in Zone 4.

How to protect plants

There are no hard and fast rules to wintering plants over. A lot depends upon the local climate and where your balcony, courtyard, or rooftop is located. Winter winds are often as hazardous as seesaw temperatures. Plants that have to endure icy cold gales, high on an exposed balcony, are obviously going to be far more affected by plummeting temperatures than their cousins ensconced in a ground-floor courtyard, shielded from the elements.

However, experienced balcony gardeners agree that it's worth giving valuable trees, shrubs, and perennials some form of protection once winter comes. One condo green thumb, who lives eight floors up and has never lost a plant during the cold months in her northern city, recommends this routine (which she follows religiously every year):

Do
✓ Start putting your garden to bed early in the fall, because it will take longer than you think.
✓ Tackle houseplants first. If pots aren't too big and cumbersome, remove the plant, scrape soil off their roots, and give the entire plant a "plunge" bath in a plastic basin or bucket. (Use a mild product like Dove, not detergent.) Rinse everything off thoroughly, then leave it to dry outside on a warm day.
✓ If plants are too large for this procedure, slosh a stream of water from a garden hose through them for ten minutes. Or put them in the bathtub and turn the shower on. This laundry routine is an admitted chore, but it does help prevent infestations of bugs like spider mites during the long winter months indoors.
✓ Wash all houseplant containers too, then dry them and refill with fresh growing medium. Repot the plants and bring them inside.

- ✓ Cut down climbing annuals, like sweet potato vine, morning glories, licorice vine, and runner beans. Empty all annuals into garbage bags. Wash their pots and put them away. Take the bags to a neighborhood composting facility (or find a friend who'll compost the stuff for you).
- ✓ Trim back potted perennial herbs, such as rosemary and oregano, then bring them indoors to a sunny window ledge. Do this with basil too, but it's an annual and won't last long. When basil stems get woody, throw the plant out.
- ✓ Keep container-grown perennial vines, upright plants, and shrubs on the balcony *as long as you possibly can*. Water regularly until growth has died down, but don't fertilize. Then hill up earth around anything that's trained up walls.

Try double-potting

Buy some Styrofoam picnic coolers at the end of summer, when they're on sale. Store small potted perennials inside them, nestled in packing peanuts.

- ✓ Rose bushes: Persuade a friend with a ground-floor garden to winter them over for you. Don't remove roses from containers; simply sink the whole thing into a flowerbed to ground level and cover with a 6 in./15 cm mulch of leaves or cocoa bean hulls. (Canadian shrub roses with the brand names Explorer and Morden are tougher than hybrid tea roses and can often stay on balconies year-round without going through this procedure. But it's a good idea to wrap them. See below.)
- ✓ Perennials: Don't cut the dead foliage back unless it's very messy. (Wait till spring. It will protect the plants.) Group their containers close together in a sheltered spot, preferably close to a southern wall, where they can pick up warmth from the winter sun. Wrap containers of any perennials that may be frost-sensitive in bubble wrap or plastic sheeting. Then tuck a thick layer of an insulating

material—packing peanuts, newspapers, leaves, even pink fiberglass "wool" insulation—between the pot sides and the layer of plastic. Add a 6 in./15 cm "icing" of mulch—leaves, cocoa bean hulls, or composted sheep manure—on top of each container. In windy areas, weigh this layer down with Christmas tree branches, planks, or bricks.

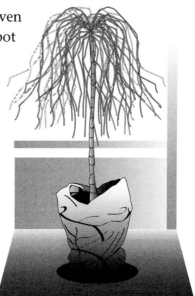

✓ Shrubs and trees: Wrap columnar ones in burlap or plastic netting. Two new products—Arbotec and Bush Jacket—are also good for protecting plants (look for them in garden centres). Group containers closely together for protection, if they aren't too heavy to move. Then follow the same procedure as for perennials. Give everything a good final soak.

✓ Wash off concrete or wood balcony ornaments and store them indoors.

✓ Clean up garden furniture and move them inside if they're made of plastic or resin. (Aluminum, wrought iron, and teak can remain on the balcony.)

✓ Drain fountains and faucets.

✓ Periodically throughout the winter, go out onto the balcony and dump a pail of room temperature water onto the container-grown perennials, shrubs, and trees. Horticulturalists used to advocate leaving dormant plants untouched during the freezing months, but they now say that the drying effects of winter can suck the moisture right out of roots.

✓ In early spring, remove containers' winter wrappings when the soil is starting to thaw. You'll know it's the right time when you can stick a finger into the soil to a depth of about 1 in./3 cm. Water thoroughly and fertilize.

Don't

✗ Try to do everything in one day.

✗ Ignore outdoor plants once winter descends. Check on them periodically. You may need to brush wet snow off branches or adjust wrapping material that has come loose.

Detecting frost damage

Exterior signs are easy to spot in spring. Trees or shrubs may have brown leaves and/or dried-out branches and twigs. Brown, falling needles on conifers are another dead giveaway. What's harder to discern is root damage. If a tree or shrub that was healthy the previous year fails to send out new buds in spring (or the buds are few and far between), it's probably been zapped by the frost.

Many container-planted specimens won't recover from winter's icy grip—but don't be in too much of a hurry to throw them out. Some can be remarkably resilient. Trim all the dead branches and twigs off, water well, and wait. You may be surprised by new shoots later on in the season.

Your own live Christmas tree

It *is* possible to cultivate one on a balcony, with a bit of effort. Here's how:

❄ Buy an evergreen already planted in a papier-mâché pot (it looks like rough brown cardboard) a few weeks before the big day. Best bets are a dwarf Alberta spruce (*Picea glauca conica*) or a Scots pine (*Pinus sylvestris*). (Avoid cedars and firs. They won't take kindly to being brought indoors.)

❄ Leave the tree out on the balcony for a couple of weeks. Water every few days with a big bucket. Then bring your Christmas showpiece into the living room for a maximum of seven to ten days. While it's inside, stand the tree on a big plastic tray, water daily, and pick a spot that's as cool as possible. Use miniature Christmas lights. (They generate less heat than big ones.)

❄ With the turkey and eggnog over, put the tree (still in its papier-mâché pot) inside a larger pot. Add some kind of insulation, evenly distributed between the layers of the two pots (see above). Store next to a wall of your building, not in an exposed area.

❄ In spring, remove winter wrappings and pot up in a bigger container. Fertilize with a water-soluble fertilizer in a formula like 20-20-20. Trim off any dead bits. Watch it grow throughout the summer. Then, if you're lucky, bring it indoors again the following holiday season. Some conifers will last for years given this treatment.

Making poinsettias last

Summer and fall have faded away. The outdoor garden is put to bed. How to import a bit of color indoors?

Many condo and apartment dwellers plump for poinsettias. These popular plants, originally from Mexico, have become indelibly associated in the minds of North Americans with the Christmas season—and we buy millions of them.

Here's how to make a poinsettia last past December:

* Don't leave it sitting in the car while you go Christmas shopping. Tropical poinsettias can take a maximum of twenty minutes outside in winter conditions. Even carrying them out to the parking lot is hazardous. Always make sure they are wrapped in a protective sleeve and a layer of paper.
* Put it in bright light, but not direct sunshine.
* Keep it away from cold windows, drafts, and heating vents. The ideal room temperature is 55 to 70°F/12 to 20°C.
* Don't let it dry out. A good deep watering every few days is best.
* If the pot is wrapped in foil, pierce a few holes in the bottom. Put a tray under the pot. Don't leave water sitting underneath.
* Keep the plant away from kids and pets. It's not poisonous, but if nibbled on, it may upset tummies.
* When the vivid scarlet starts to fade (as it inevitably will), forget trying to bring the color back. For most gardeners, the procedure is too complicated. Experts do it in greenhouses equipped with blackout curtains, but we're better off buying new plants every holiday season.

> **Hot tip**
> "In fall, don't throw out perennials that are borderline hardy, because they can surprise you. Fountain grass has survived on my balcony in mild winters."
> —*Sue Martin, northern rooftop gardener*

Where to Go for More Information

Surf the Web

Use a search engine like Google, and simply type in the words "container gardening." You'll be promptly deluged with dozens of places to look for more information.

Some of this information is useful. A lot isn't. Many gardening Web sites are simply promoting products. Along with all the hype, they sometimes offer good gardening tips, but these are often badly written and hard to read. Tracking down genuinely useful material is difficult and time-consuming. However, try:

www.windowbox.com: This site carries down-to-earth gardening tips, geared especially for container gardeners. Their advice guru is called Dr. Botnic, and he delivers his messages in a short, punchy style. Well worth checking out.

www.suite101.com/gardencenter: A general gardening Web site that includes a section on container gardening. Sometimes useful.

www.citygardening.net: Covers all types of gardening, but has some items of interest.

www.icangarden.com: An award-winning Web site with solid gardening information. Much of it is aimed at people with bigger gardens, but there are sometimes tips on container gardening.

Ask a Master Gardener

Master Gardeners are trained volunteers who take courses in horticulture. They spend much of their spare time educating the public about gardening, simply because they love it so much.

You'll find Master Gardeners in information booths at flower shows and agricultural shows. In many cities, they also run gardening information phone lines, which provide free answers to gardening questions.

To find out if there's a Master Gardener group operating in your area, ask your local horticultural society or garden center.

Get to know other gardeners

If you live in a condominium or apartment building, get a gardening group going. Swap ideas, plants, and tips. Local green thumbs are by far the best sources of practical information about gardening in your area. Another good bet is to join a local horticultural society. Garden centers usually know how to get in touch with them.

Acknowledgments

Gardeners have to be the most generous people on earth. I've had the good fortune to meet dozens of them in the course of writing a column on condo gardening for a major North American newspaper. In every instance, these individuals were delighted to share with me their knowledge, creative ideas, and, often, their plants. I have headed home clutching seeds, cuttings, and green garbage bags stuffed full of stems and roots (hastily dug up for my benefit), with the gardener's classic admonition, "You simply *must* try this plant!" ringing in my ears.

Without the enthusiastic advice of so many open-hearted souls, I could not have written this book. In particular, I am grateful to Sue Martin, whose jewel of a garden, on a condo balcony, provided much inspiration. Thanks are also due to a long list of contributors. They include: Steve Aikenhead, Mara Arndt, Kenneth Brown, Dugald Cameron, Christopher Cantlon, Cathie Cox, Ann Dobec, Susan Dyer, Denis Flanagan, Tony Fleishmann, Gwen Farrow, Mark Hartley, Wendy Humphries, Martin Knirr, Nona Koivula, Anne Kotyk, Debbie Kucheran, Anna Leggatt, Dominique Leonard, Jack Lieber, Ross McKean, Mary-Fran McQuade, George Makrygiannis, Shirley Martin, Bev Mitchell, Ellen Moorhouse, Vera Muth, Ben Ng, Catherine Pitt, Kim Price, Jennifer Reynolds, Conrad Richter, Larry Sherk, Athina Smardenka, Yoga Thiyagarajah, Mary Lu Toms, Pauline Walsh, Ida Weippert, Dave Wilson, Karen York, and Elsa Young.

I also wish to thank Barrie Murdock for his expertise in scanning (and vastly improving) my photographs, and editor Sue Sumeraj for her suggestions on improving the text.

Index